MILITARY AVIATION LIBRARY
World War II
United States
Aircraft

MILITARY AVIATION LIBRARY
World War II
United States
Aircraft

Bill Gunston

CHARTWELL
BOOKS, INC.

Published by Chartwell Books Inc., New York

©Salamander Books Ltd., 1985

Colour profiles, cutaways and three-view drawings © Pilot Press Ltd.

ISBN: 0 89009 898 0

PICTURE CREDITS

Bell Aerospace: 10 (bottom), 11 (top).
Convair (General Dynamics): 20.
Fairchild Republic: 58
Bill Gunston Collection: 43 (top), 56 (top).
Imperial War Museum: 21 (bottom left), 61.
J. MacClancy Collection: 10 (top), 16 (top), 26, 27, 30 (top), 45, 50 (top), 59.
McDonnell Douglas: 32, 33 (bottom).
Jerry Miller: 60 (bottom).
J. G. Moore Collection: 14, 23 (bottom), 31 (top), 44, 49.
Pilot Press Ltd: 29 (top), 46 (bottom).
Paul Popper: 43 (bottom).
Stato Maggiore Aeronautica: 48 (top).
US Air Force: 11 (bottom), 15 (top), 16 (bottom), 17, 31 (bottom), 33 (top), 34 (top), 35 (top), 47 (bottom), 50 (bottom), 53, 54, 57.
US Air Force (J. MacClancy Collection): 8, 13, 15 (bottom).
US Air Force (J. Scutts Collection): 19, 56 (bottom).
US Navy: 21 (bottom right), 28, 29 (bottom), 30 (bottom), 34 (bottom), 46 (top), 47 (top), 48 (bottom), 60 (top).
US Navy (J. MacClancy Collection). 23 (top), 42.
US Navy (J. Scutts Collection). 35 (bottom), 43 (centre).

Contents

Bell P-39 Airacobra

P-39 to P39Q Airacobra (data for P-39L)

Origin: Bell Aircraft Corporation.
Type: Single-seat fighter.
Engine: 1,325hp Allison V-1710-63 vee-12 liquid-cooled.
Dimensions: Span 34ft 0in (10·37m); length 30ft 2in (9·2m); height (one prop-blade vertical) 11ft 10in (3·63m).
Weights: Empty 5,600lb (2540kg); loaded 7,780lb (3530kg).
Performance: Maximum speed 380mph (612km/h); initial climb 4,000ft (1220m)/min; service ceiling 35,000ft (10,670m); ferry range with drop tank at 160mph (256km/h) 1,475 miles (2360km).
Armament: One 37mm cannon with 30 rounds (twice as many as in first sub-types), two synchronised 0·5in Colt-Brownings and two or four 0·30in in outer wings.
History: First flight of XP-39 August 1939; (P-39F to M-sub-types, 1942); final batch (P-39Q) May 1944.
Users: France, Italy (CB), Portugal, Soviet Union, UK (RAF, briefly), US (AAF).

Development: First flown as a company prototype in 1939, this design by R. J. Woods and O. L. Woodson was unique in having a nosewheel-type landing gear and the engine behind the pilot. The propeller was driven by a long shaft under the pilot's seat and a reduction gearbox in the nose, the latter also containing a big 37mm cannon firing through the propeller hub. Other guns were also fitted in the nose, the first production aircraft, the P-39C of 1941, having two 0·30in and two 0·5in all synchronised to fire past the propeller. Britain ordered the unconventional fighter in 1940 and in June 1941 the first Airacobra I arrived, with the 37mm gun and 15 rounds having been replaced by a 20mm Hispano with 60. Two 0·303in Brownings

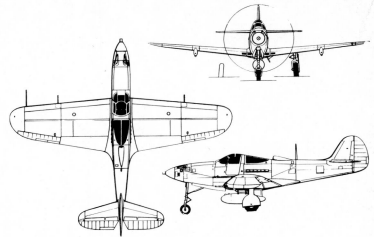

Above: Three-view of P-39Q with drop tank.

in the nose and four more in the wings completed the armament. No 601 Sqn did poorly with it and failed to keep the unusual aircraft serviceable, but the US Army Air Force used it in big numbers. Altogether 9,588 were built and used with fair success in the Mediterranean and Far East, some 5,000 being supplied to the Soviet Union, mainly through Iran. Biggest production version was the P-39Q, of which over 4,900 were built. The P-39 was succeeded in production in 1944 by the P-63 Kingcobra.

Left: The P-39L was an interim aircraft with Curtiss Electric propeller (data above apply). This one served with 91st FS, 81st FG.

Left: This Bell P-400 was a requisitioned British P-39, impressed into USAAC service still with the 20mm gun fitted, and with British serial number still showing.

Below: These are P-39Ds; the photograph was taken before mid-1942. The most numerous (Q) P-39 had no guns inside the wings.

Above: The exhaust stubs above the wings, rather than in the normal position on the sides of the forward fuselage, and the carburettor intake immediately aft of the cockpit, indicate the unusual mid-fuselage location of the P-39's engine. The propeller was driven by means of a long extension shaft and a reduction gearbox to allow a 37mm cannon to be mounted in the nose, firing through the propeller hub; two 0·5in machine-guns were also mounted in the nose, and the P-39D illustrated also had four 0·303in machine guns in the wings.

Right: P-39Ds in formation. The similar model ordered for the RAF featured a revised armament of a 20mm cannon and six 0·303in machine guns, but performance was disappointing and most of those ordered were passed on to Russia or returned to the USAAF, which designated the ex-RAF models P-400.

Below: Although rejected by the RAF as inferior to the Spitfire and Hurricane, the P-39 was used in large numbers by the USAAF. Many were sent to the Pacific following the attack on Pearl Harbor, and others fought in Italy: in both theatres they were particularly useful for close support and ground attack work, the ventral rack carrying bombs of up to 500lb (227kg).

Bell P-59 Airacomet

YP-59, P-59A and XF2L-1

Origin: Bell Aircraft Corporation.
Type: Single-seat jet fighter trainer.
Engines: Two 2,000lb (907kg) thrust General Electric J31-GE-3 turbojets.
Dimensions: Span 45ft 6in (13·87m); length 38ft 1½in (11·63m); height 12ft 0in (3·66m).
Weights: Empty 7,950lb (3610kg); loaded 12,700lb (5760kg).
Performance: Maximum speed 413mph (671km/h); service ceiling 46,200ft (14,080m); maximum range with two 125 Imp gal drop tanks 520 miles (837km) at 289mph (465km/h) at 20,000ft (6096m).
Armament: Usually none, but some YP-59A fitted with nose guns (eg one 37mm cannon and three 0·5in) and one rack under each wing for bomb as alternative to drop tank.
History: First flight (XP-59A) 1 October 1942; (production P-59A) 7 August 1944.
Users: US (AAF, Navy); (one UK in exchange for Meteor I).

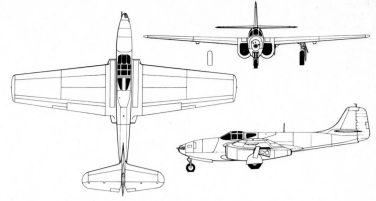

Above: Three-view of P-59A; P-59B was identical but had 55 Imp gal extra fuel capacity.

Development: In June 1941 the US government and General "Hap" Arnold of the Army Air Corps were told of Britain's development of the turbojet engine. On 5 September 1941 Bell Aircraft was requested to design a jet fighter and in the following month a Whittle turbojet, complete engineering drawings and a team from Power Jets Ltd arrived from Britain to hasten proceedings. The result was that Bell flew the first American jet in one year from the start of work. The Whittle-type centrifugal engines, Americanised and made by General Electric as the 1,100lb (500kg) thrust 1-A, were installed under the wing roots, close to the centreline and easily accessible (two were needed to fly an aircraft of useful size). Flight development went extremely smoothly, and 12 YP-59As for service trials were delivered in 1944. Total procurement amounted to 66 only, including three XF2L-1s for the US Navy, and the P-59A was classed as a fighter-trainer because it was clear it would not make an effective front-line fighter. But in comparison with the fast timescale it was a remarkable achievement, performance being very similar to that attained with the early Meteors.

Left: One of the first three XP-59 prototypes, seen on the desert at Muroc where Edwards AFB now fills the landscape.

Right: Rolling an XP-59A back to the apron after an early test. Elaborate precautions were taken to preserve secrecy, to the point of fitting a dummy propeller to the first XP-59A shipped to Muroc by rail in September 1942.

Bell P-63 Kingcobra

P-63A to E and RP-63

Origin: Bell Aircraft Corporation, Buffalo, NY.
Type: Single-seat fighter-bomber.
Engine: One Allison V-1710 vee-12 liquid-cooled, (A) 1,500hp (war emergency rating) V-1710-93, (C) 1,800hp V-1710-117.
Dimensions: Span 38ft 4in (11·68m); length 32ft 8in (9·96m); height 12ft 7in (3·84m).
Weights: Empty (A) 6,375lb (2892kg); maximum (A) 10,500lb (4763kg).
Performance: Maximum speed (all) 410mph (660km/h); typical range with three bombs 340 miles (547km); ferry range with three tanks 2,575 miles (4143km).
Armament: Usually one 37mm and four 0·5in, plus up to three 500lb (227kg) bombs.
History: First flight 7 December 1942; service delivery October 1943; final delivery early 1945.
Users: Brazil, France, Italy, Soviet Union, US (AAF).

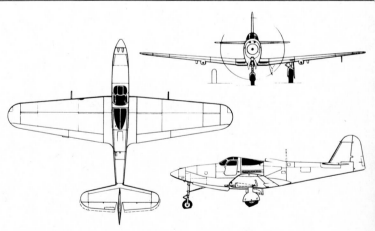

Above: Three-view of P-63A (all except D similar).

Development: Though it looked like a P-39 with a different tail, in fact the P-63 was a completely different design, greatly improved in the light of painful combat experience. It fully met a February 1941 Army requirement, but air war developed so fast that — though Bell did a competent job to a fast schedule — the P-63 was outclassed before it reached the squadrons. It never fought with the US forces, but 2,421 of the 3,303 built went to the Soviet Union where their tough airframes and good close-support capability made them popular. At least 300 went to the Free French, in both A and C variants (both of which had a wealth of sub-types). The D had a sliding bubble canopy and larger wing, and the E extra fuel. The only USAAF Kingcobras were 332 completed or modified as heavily armoured RP-63A or C manned target aircraft, shot at by live "frangible" (easily shattered) bullets. Each hit made a powerful lamp light at the tip of the spinner.

Left: A Kingcobra in USAAF markings, probably a P-63A-6 with bomb racks outboard of the wing guns.

Right: Bell's plant at Buffalo delivered well over 2,000 Kingcobras to the Soviet Union, where they stood up well to the harsh environment. Here are a few hundred at Buffalo.

Right: Side elevation of the 16th aircraft, strictly a P-59A but still without armament. Most early P-59 aircraft later were used for various trials programmes. One was shipped to England, where it was taken on charge as RJ362/G (called "Bell 27 Airacomet") in exchange for one of the first Meteors which was shipped to Muroc and checked out there by John Grierson.

Boeing B-17 Fortress

Model 299, Y1B-17 and B-17 to B-17G (basic data for G)

Origin: Boeing Airplane Company, Seattle; also built by Vega Aircraft Corporation, Burbank, and Douglas Aircraft Company, Tulsa.
Type: High-altitude bomber, with crew of six to ten.
Engines: Four 1,200hp Wright R-1820-97 (B-17C to E, R-1820-65) Cyclone nine-cylinder radials with exhaust-driven turbochargers.
Dimensions: Span 103ft 9in (31·6m): length 74ft 9in (22·8m); (B-17B, C, D) 67ft 11in; (B-17E) 73ft 10in; height 19ft 1in (5·8m); (B-17B, C, D) 15ft 5in.
Weights: Empty 32,720–35,800lb (14,855–16,200kg); (B-17B, C, D) typically 31,150lb; maximum loaded 65,600lb (29,700kg) (B-17B, C, D) 44,200–46,650lb; (B-17E) 53,000lb.
Performance: Maximum speed 287mph (462km/h); (B-17C, D) 323mph; (B-17E) 317mph; cruising speed 182mph (293km/h); (B-17C, D) 250mph; (B-17E) 210mph; service ceiling 35,000ft (10,670m); range 1,100 miles (1,760km) with maximum bomb load (other versions up to 3,160 miles with reduced weapon load).
Armament: Twin 0·5in Brownings in chin, dorsal, ball and tail turrets, plus two in nose sockets, one in radio compartment and one in each waist position. Normal internal bomb load 6,000lb (2724kg), but maximum 12,800lb (5800kg).
History: First flight (299) 28 July 1935; (Y1B-17) January 1937; first delivery (B-17B) June 1939; final delivery April 1945.
Users: UK (RAF), US (AAC/AAF, Navy).

Above: Three-view of B-17G.

Below: The subject of the cutaway is the B-17F, the first model made in truly vast quantity (3,405) and second in importance only to the G of which 8,680 were made. Item 59 was often a 0.5in gun.

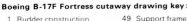

Boeing B-17F Fortress cutaway drawing key:

1 Rudder construction
2 Rudder tab
3 Rudder tab actuation
4 Tail gunner's station
5 Gunsight
6 Twin 0·5-in (12,7-mm) machine guns
7 Tail cone
8 Tail gunner's seat
9 Ammunition troughs
10 Elevator trim tab
11 Starboard elevator
12 Tailplane structure
13 Tailplane front spar
14 Tailplane/fuselage attachment
15 Control cables
16 Elevator control mechanism
17 Rudder control linkage
18 Rudder post
19 Rudder centre hinge
20 Fin structure
21 Rudder upper hinge
22 Fin skinning
23 Aerial attachment
24 Aerials
25 Fin leading-edge de-icing boot
26 Port elevator
27 Port tailplane
28 Tailplane leading-edge de-icing boot
29 Dorsal fin structure
30 Fuselage frame
31 Tailwheel actuation
32 Toilet
33 Tailwheel (retracted) fairing
34 Fully-swivelling retractable tailwheel
35 Crew entry door
36 Control cables
37 Starboard waist hatch
38 Starboard waist 0·5-in (12,7-mm) machine gun
39 Gun support frame
40 Ammunition box
41 Ventral aerial
42 Waist gunners' positions
43 Port waist 0·5-in (12,7-mm) machine gun
44 Ceiling control cable runs
45 Dorsal aerial mast
46 Ball turret stanchion support
47 Ball turret stanchion
48 Ball turret actuation mechanism
49 Support frame
50 Ball turret roof
51 Twin 0·5-in (12,7-mm) machine guns
52 Ventral ball turret
53 Wingroot fillet
54 Bulkhead
55 Radio operator's compartment
56 Camera access hatch
57 Radio compartment windows (port and starboard)
58 Ammunition boxes
59 Single 0·3-in (7,62-mm) dorsal machine gun
60 Radio compartment roof glazing
61 Radio compartment/bomb-bay bulkhead
62 Fire extinguisher
63 Radio operator's station (port side)
64 Handrail links
65 Bulkhead step
66 Wing rear spar/fuselage attachment
67 Wingroot profile
68 Bomb-bay central catwalk
69 Vertical bomb stowage racks (starboard installation shown)
70 Horizontal bomb stowage (port side shown)
71 Dinghy stowage
72 Twin 0·5-in (12,7-mm) machine guns
73 Dorsal turret
74 Port wing flaps
75 Cooling air slots
76 Aileron tab (port only)
77 Port aileron
78 Port navigation light
79 Wing skinning
80 Wing leading-edge de-icing boot
81 Port landing light
82 Wing corrugated inner skin
83 Port outer wing fuel tank (nine inter-rib cells)
84 No 1 engine nacelle
85 Cooling gills
86 Three-blade propellers
87 No 2 engine nacelle
88 Wing leading-edge de-icing boot
89 Port mid-wing (self-sealing) fuel tanks
90 Flight deck upper glazing
91 Flight deck/bomb-bay bulkhead
92 Oxygen cylinders
93 Co-pilot's seat
94 Co-pilot's control column
95 Headrest/armour
96 Compass installation
97 Pilot's seat
98 Windscreen
99 Central control console pedestal
100 Side windows
101 Navigation equipment
102 Navigator's compartment upper window (subsequently replaced by ceiling astrodome)
103 Navigator's table
104 Side gun mounting
105 Enlarged cheek windows (flush)
106 Ammunition box
107 Bombardier's panel
108 Norden bombsight installation
109 Plexiglass frameless nose-cone
110 Single 0·5-in (12,7-mm) nose machine gun
111 Optically-flat bomb-aiming panel
112 Pitot head fairing (port and starboard)
113 D/F loop bullet fairing
114 Port mainwheel
115 Flight deck underfloor control linkage

Above: A B-17G-25 of the 8th Air Force's 96th Bomb Group, based at Snetterton Heath, England.

116 Wingroot/fuselage fairing
117 Wing front spar/fuselage attachment
118 Battery access panels (wingroot leading-edge)
119 No 3 engine nacelle spar bulkhead
120 Intercooler pressure duct
121 Mainwheel well
122 Oil tank (nacelle inboard wall)

123 Nacelle structure
124 Exhaust
125 Retracted mainwheel (semi-recessed)
126 Firewall
127 Cooling gills
128 Exhaust collector ring assembly
129 Three-blade propellers
130 Undercarriage retraction struts
131 Starboard mainwheel
132 Axle
133 Mainwheel oleo leg
134 Propeller reduction gear casing
135 1,000 hp Wright R-1820-65 radial engine
136 Exhaust collector ring
137 Engine upper bearers
138 Firewall
139 Engine lower bearers

140 Intercooler assembly
141 Oil tank (nacelle outboard wall)
142 Supercharger
143 Intake
144 Supercharger waste-gate
145 Starboard landing light
146 Supercharger intake
147 Intercooler intake
148 Ducting
149 No 4 engine nacelle spar bulkhead
150 Oil radiator intake
151 Main spar web structure
152 Mid-wing fuel tank rib cut-outs
153 Auxiliary mid spar
154 Rear spar
155 Landing flap profile
156 Cooling air slots
157 Starboard outer wing fuel tank (nine inter-rib cells)

158 Flap structure
159 Starboard aileron
160 Outboard wing ribs
161 Spar assembly
162 Wing leading-edge de-icing boot
163 Aileron control linkage
164 Wing corrugated inner skin
165 Wingtip structure
166 Starboard navigation light

Above: Olive-drab B-17Fs thunder aloft in 1942. Later the 8th AAF "Forts" were distinguished by unit insignia readable from a distance; and they were delivered unpainted, because the trail-streaming formations could be seen 100 miles away.

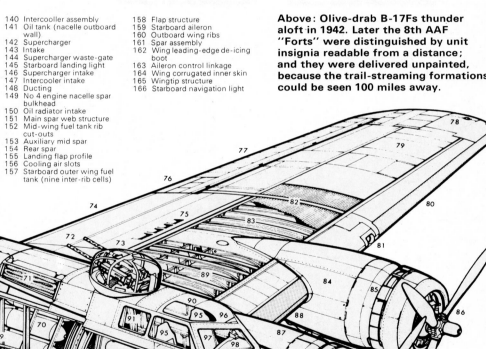

►**Development:** In May 1934 the US Army Air Corps issued a specification for a multi-engined anti-shipping bomber to defend the nation against enemy fleets. The answer was expected to be similar to the Martin B-10, but Boeing proposed four engines in order to carry the same bomb load faster and higher. It was a huge financial risk for the Seattle company but the resulting Model 299 was a giant among combat aircraft, with four 750hp Pratt & Whitney Hornet engines, a crew of eight and stowage for eight 600lb (272kg) bombs internally.

Above: "Stop" waves a ground-crewman to the skipper of a red-tailed G-model on the green grass of a British base.

Left: Last-minute check before a mission by an RAF Coastal Command Fortress IIA (B-17E). Some 200 served from mid-1942.

at 232mph, causing editors to think of the Flying Fortress in a new light. The service-test batch of 13 Y1B-17 adopted the Wright Cyclone engine, later versions all being turbocharged for good high-altitude performance. The production B-17B introduced a new nose and bigger rudder and flaps, though the wing loading was conservative and an enduring characteristic of every "Fort" was sedate flying.

With the B-17C came a ventral bathtub, flush side guns, armour and self-sealing tanks. In return for combat data 20 were supplied to the RAF, which used them on a few high-altitude daylight raids with 90 Sqn of Bomber Command. It was found that the Norden sight tended to malfunction, the

Boeing B-29 Superfortress
Model 345, B-29 to -29C

Origin: Boeing Airplane Company, Seattle, Renton and Wichita; also built by Bell Aircraft, Marietta, and Glenn L. Martin Company, Omaha.
Type: High-altitude heavy bomber, with crew of 10–14.
Engines: Four 2,200hp Wright R-3350-23 Duplex Cyclone 18-cylinder radials each with two exhaust-driven turbochargers.
Dimensions: Span 141ft 3in (43·05m); length 99ft (30·2m); height 27ft 9in (8·46m).
Weights: Empty 74,500lb (33,795kg); loaded 135,000lb (61,240kg).
Performance: Maximum speed 357mph (575km/h) at 30,000ft (9144m); cruising speed 290mph (467km/h); climb to 25,000ft (7620m) in 43min; service ceiling 36,000ft (10,973m); range with 10,000lb (4540kg) bombs 3,250miles (5230km).
Armament: Four GE twin-0·50in turrets above and below, sighted from nose or three waist sighting stations; Bell tail turret, with own gunner, with one 20mm cannon and twin 0·50in; internal bomb load up to 20,000lb (9072kg). Carried first two nuclear bombs. With modification, carried two 22,000lb British bombs externally under inner wings.
History: First flight 21 September 1942; (pre-production YB-29) 26 June 1943); squadron delivery July 1943; first combat mission 5 June 1944; last delivery May 1946.
User: US (AAF, Navy).

Development and mass production of the B-29, the Boeing Model 345, was one of the biggest tasks in the history of aviation. It began with a March 1938 study for a new bomber with pressurised cabin and tricycle landing gear. This evolved into the 345 and in August 1940 money was voted for two prototypes. In January 1942 the Army Air Force ordered 14 YB-29s and 500 production aircraft. By February, while Boeing engineers worked night and day on the huge technical problems, a production organisation was set up involving Boeing, Bell, North American and Fisher (General Motors). Martin came in later and by VJ-day more than 3,000 Superforts

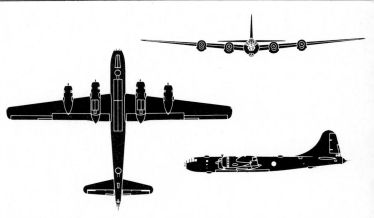

Above: Three-view of B-29 (two-gun forward dorsal turret).

had been delivered. This was a fantastic achievement because each represented five or six times the technical effort of any earlier bomber. In engine power, gross weight, wing loading, pressurisation, armament, airborne systems and even basic structure the B-29 set a wholly new standard. First combat mission was flown by the 58th Bomb Wing on 5 June 1944, and by 1945 20 groups from the Marianas were sending 500 B-29s at a time to flatten and burn Japan's cities. (Three aircraft made emergency landings in Soviet territory, and Tupolev's design bureau put the design into production as the Tu-4 bomber and Tu-70 transport.) The -29C had all guns except those in the tail removed, increasing speed and altitude. After the war there were 19 variants of B-29, not including the Washington B.I supplied to help the RAF in 1950–58.

Left: One of the most famous Superforts was the unarmed "special" Enola Gay which on 6 August 1945 dropped the first atom bomb on Hiroshima.

Right: The first production B-29s were painted, but this was soon abandoned.

Browning guns to freeze at the high altitude and German fighters to attack from astern in a defensive blind spot. While surviving Fortress Is operated with Coastal and Middle East forces, the improved B-17D joined the US Army and bore the brunt of early fighting in the Pacific. But extensive combat experience led to the redesigned B-17E, with powered dorsal, ventral (ball) and tail turrets, a huge fin for high-altitude bombing accuracy and much more armour and equipment. This went into mass production by Boeing, Lockheed-Vega and Douglas-Tulsa. It was the first weapon of the US 8th Bomber Command in England and on 17 August 1942 began three gruelling years of day strategic bombing in Europe.

Soon the E gave way to the B-17F, of which 3,405 were built, with many detail improvements, including a long Plexiglas nose, paddle-blade propellers and provision for underwing racks. At the end of 1942 came the final bomber model, the B-17G, with chin turret and flush staggered waist guns. A total of 8,680 G models were made, Boeing's Seattle plant alone turning out 16 a day, and the total B-17 run amounted to 12,731. A few B-17Fs

Above: A sight to quicken the pulse! Sections of G-models from the 381st BG outward bound from Ridgewell, escorted by a lone P-51B Mustang. This group dropped 22,160 tons of bombs.

were converted to XB-40s, carrying extra defensive guns to help protect the main Bomb Groups, while at least 25 were turned into BQ-7 Aphrodite radio-controlled missiles loaded with 12,000lb of high explosive for use against U-boat shelters. Many F and G models were fitted with H_2X radar with the scanner retracting into the nose or rear fuselage, while other versions included the F-9 reconnaissance, XC-108 executive transport, CB-17 utility transport, PB-1W radar early-warning, PB-1G lifeboat-carrying air/sea rescue and QB-17 target drone. After the war came other photo, training, drone-director, search/rescue and research versions, including many used as engine and equipment testbeds. In 1970, 25 years after first flight, one of many civil Forts used for agricultural or forest-fire protection was re-engined with Dart turboprops!

Boeing Stearman

Model 75 Kaydet, PT-13, -17, -18, -27, N2S

Origin: Boeing Airplane Company (see text).
Type: Dual-control primary trainer.
Engine: 215hp Lycoming R-680-5 (PT-13, N2S-2, -5); 220hp Continental R-670-5 (PT-17, PT-27, N2S-1, -3, -4); 225hp Jacobs R-755 (PT-18) radials, R-680 having nine cylinders, others seven.
Dimensions: Span 32ft 2in (9.8m); length 25ft 0½in (7.63m); height 9ft 2in (2.79m).
Weights: Empty about 1,936lb (878kg); loaded 2,717–2,810lb (1232–1275kg).
Performance: Maximum speed 120–126mph (193–203km/h); initial climb 840ft (256m)/min; service ceiling 11,200ft (3413m); range 440–505 miles (708–812km).
Armament: Only on Model 76D export versions, typically two 0.30in machine guns in lower wings and single 0.30in aimed by observer in rear cockpit. Optional racks for light bombs under fuselage.
History: First flight (Model 70) December 1933; (Model 75) early 1936; final delivery February 1945.
Users: US (AAC/AAF, Navy, Marines) and at least 25 other air forces.

Above: Three-view of typical Boeing Stearman trainer.

Development: When the monopolistic United Aircraft and Transport combine was broken up by the government in 1934, the Stearman Aircraft Co remained a subsidiary of Boeing and in 1939 the Wichita plant lost the Stearman name entirely. Yet the family of trainers built by Boeing to Floyd Stearman's design have always been known by the designer's name rather than that of the maker. The Model 70 biplane trainer was conservative and, as it emerged when biplanes were fast disappearing from combat aviation, it might have been a failure — especially as Claude Ryan had a trim mono-plane trainer competing for orders. Yet the result was the biggest production of any biplane in history prior to today's An-2, as the chief primary trainer in North America in World War II. The Model 70 flew on a 220hp Lycoming but the Navy, the first customer, bought 61 NS-1 primary trainers (Model 73) with surplus 225hp Wright Whirlwinds drawn from storage. By 1941 Boeing had delivered 17 similar aircraft and 78 Model 76s (with various engines) for export. But the main production type was the Model 75, ordered by the Army Air Corps after evaluating the first example in 1936. The first were PT-13s of various models, with Lycoming engines of 215 to 280hp, but the biggest family was the PT-17. The 300 built for the RCAF were named Kaydets, a name unofficially adopted for the entire series. A few Canadian PT-27 Kaydets and similar Navy N2S-5s had enclosed cockpits. Total production, including spares, was 10,346, of which several hundred are still flying, mainly as glider tugs and crop dusters.

Left: Primary trainers of the US Navy were doped all-yellow. Various types of NS and N2S Stearmans were the Navy's standard primary trainers of World War II.

Consolidated Vultee Model 32 B-24 Liberator

For variants, see text
(data for B-24J Liberator B.VI)

Origin: Consolidated Vultee Aircraft Corporation; also built by Douglas, Ford and North American Aviation.
Type: Long-range bomber with normal crew of ten.
Engines: Four 1,200hp Pratt & Whitney R-1830-65 Twin Wasp 14-cylinder two-row radials.
Dimensions: Span 110ft 0in (33.5m); length 67ft 2in (20.47m); height 18ft 0in (5.49m).
Weights: Empty 37,000lb (16,783kg); loaded 65,000lb (29,484kg).
Performance: Maximum speed 290mph (467km/h); initial climb 900ft (274m)/min; service ceiling 28,000ft (8534m); range at 190mph (306km/h) with 5,000lb (2268kg) bomb load 2,200 miles (3540km).
Armament: Ten 0.50in Brownings arranged in four electrically operated turrets (Consolidated or Emerson in nose, Martin dorsal, Briggs-Sperry retractable ventral "ball" and Consolidated or Motor Products tail) with two guns each plus two singles in manual waist positions; two bomb bays with roll-up doors with vertical racks on each side of central catwalk for up to 8,000lb (3629kg); two 4,000lb (1814kg) bombs could be hung externally on inner-wing racks instead of internal load.
History: First flight (XB-24) 29 December 1939; first delivery (LB-30A) March 1941; first combat service (Liberator I) June 1941; first combat service with US Army (B-24C) November 1941; termination of production 31 May 1945; withdrawal from service (various smaller air forces) 1955–56.
Users: Australia, Brazil, Canada, China, Czechoslovakia, France, India, Italy (CB), New Zealand, Portugal, South Africa, Soviet Union, Turkey, UK (RAF, BOAC), US (AAF, Navy, Marines); other countries post-war.

Development: This distinctive aircraft was one of the most important in the history of aviation. Conceived five years after the B-17 it did not, in fact, notably improve on the older bomber's performance and in respect of engine-out performance and general stability and control it was inferior,

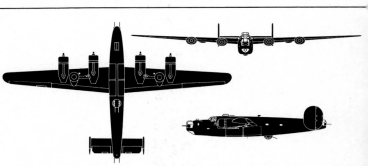

Above: Three-view of B-24H (B-24J similar except front turret).

being a handful for the average pilot. It was also by far the most complicated and expensive combat aircraft the world had seen — though in this it merely showed the way things were going to be in future. Yet it was built in bigger numbers than any other American aircraft in history, in more versions for more purposes than any other aircraft in history, and served on every front in World War II and with 15 Allied nations. In terms of industrial effort it transcended anything seen previously in any sphere of endeavour.

Right: Best chronicled of all bombing missions by the USAAF is the Ploesti (Romania) refinery attack by B-24Ds of the 44th, 93rd, 98th and 389th Bomb Groups on 1 August 1943.

Below: Bombs rain down from B-24Hs of the 487th BG.

Brewster F2A Buffalo

F2A-1 (239), F2A-2 (339), F2A-3 and 439 Buffalo 1 (data for F2A-2)

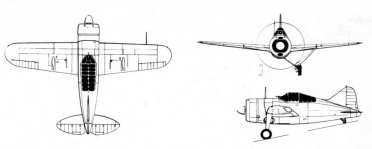

Origin: Brewster Aircraft Company, Long Island City.
Type: Single-seat carrier or land-based fighter.
Engine: 1,100hp Wright R-1820-40 (G-205A) Cyclone nine-cylinder radial.
Dimensions: Span 35ft (10·67m); length 26ft 4in (8m); height 12ft 1in (3·7m).
Weights: Empty 4,630lb (2100kg); loaded 7,055lb (3200kg) (varied from 6,848–7,159lb).
Performance: Maximum speed 300mph (483km/h); initial climb 3,070ft (935m)/min; service ceiling 30,500ft (9300m); range 650–950 miles (1045–1530km).
Armament: Four machine guns, two in fuselage and two in wing, calibre of each pair being 0·30in, 0·303in or, mostly commonly, 0·50in.
History: First flight (XF2A-1) January 1938; first service delivery April 1939; termination of production 1942.
Users: Australia, Finland, Netherlands (E. Indies), New Zealand, UK (RAF), US (Navy, Marines).

Development: The Brewster company was established in 1810 to build carriages. In 1935 it plunged into planemaking and secured an order for a US Navy scout-bomber. It also entered a competition for a carrier-based monoplane fighter and won. Not surprisingly, it took almost two years — a long time in those days — to fly the first prototype. Yet one must give the

Above: Three-view of the F2A-3, the final sub-type ordered mainly to keep the Brewster factory busy during 1941.

team their due, for the F2A-1 was confirmed as the Navy's choice for its first monoplane fighter even after Grumman had flown the G.36 (Wildcat). In June 1938 a contract was placed for 54 of these tubby mid-wingers, then armed with one 0·50 in and one 0·30in machine guns. Only 11 reached USS *Saratoga*; the rest went to Finland, where from February 1940 until the end of World War II they did extremely well. The US Navy bought 43 more powerful and more heavily armed F2A-2 (Model 339), and then 108 F2A-3 with armour and self-sealing tanks. Of these, 21 in the hands of the Marine Corps put up a heroic struggle in the first Battle of Midway. In 1939 bulk orders were placed by Belgium and Britain, and the RAF operated 170 delivered in 1941 to Singapore. Another 72 were bought by the Netherlands.

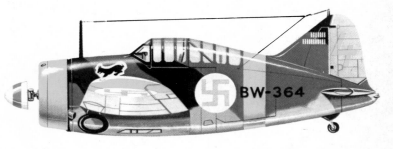

Above: A Brewster Model 239 (ex-F2A-1) of the Finnish Air Force. These fighters equipped Nos 24 and 26 Sqns of Air Regiment LeR 2, and were successful against various Soviet types.

Left: The wartime censor has deleted the code-letters of this RAF, RAAF or RNZAF squadron in Malaya (note Blenheim IV).

▶ It had a curious layout, dictated by the slender Davis wing placed above the tall bomb bays. This wing was efficient in cruising flight, which combined with great fuel capacity to give the "Lib" longer range than any other landplane of its day. But it meant that the main gears were long, and they were retracted outwards by electric motors, nearly everything on board being electric. Early versions supplied to the RAF were judged not combat-ready, and they began the Atlantic Return Ferry Service as LB-30A transports. Better defences led to the RAF Liberator I, used by Coastal Command with ASV radar and a battery of fixed 20mm cannon. The RAF Liberator II (B-24C) introduced power turrets and served as a bomber in the Middle East. The first mass-produced version was the B-24D, with turbocharged engines in oval cowls, more fuel and armament and many detail changes; 2,738 served US Bomb Groups in Europe and the Pacific, and RAF Coastal Command closed the mid-Atlantic gap, previously beyond aircraft range, where U-boat packs lurked.

Biggest production of all centred on the B-24G, H and J (Navy PB4Y and RAF B.VI and GR.VI), of which 10,208 were built. These all had four turrets, and were made by Convair, North American, Ford and Douglas. Other variants included the L and M with different tail turrets, the N with single fin, the luridly painted CB-24 lead ships, the TB-24 trainer, F-7 photo-reconnaissance, C-109 fuel tanker and QB-24 drone. There was also a complete family of Liberator Transport versions, known as C-87 Liberator Express to the Army, RY-3 to the Navy and C.VII and C.IX to the RAF, many having the huge single fin also seen on the PB4Y-2 Privateer. Excluding one-offs such as the redesigned R2Y transport and 1,800 equivalent aircraft delivered as spares, total production of all versions was a staggering 19,203. Their achievements were in proportion.

Right: A B-24J-105 of the 392nd Bombardment Group of the 8th AAF, based at Wendling, England.

Consolidated B-24J Liberator cutaway drawing key:

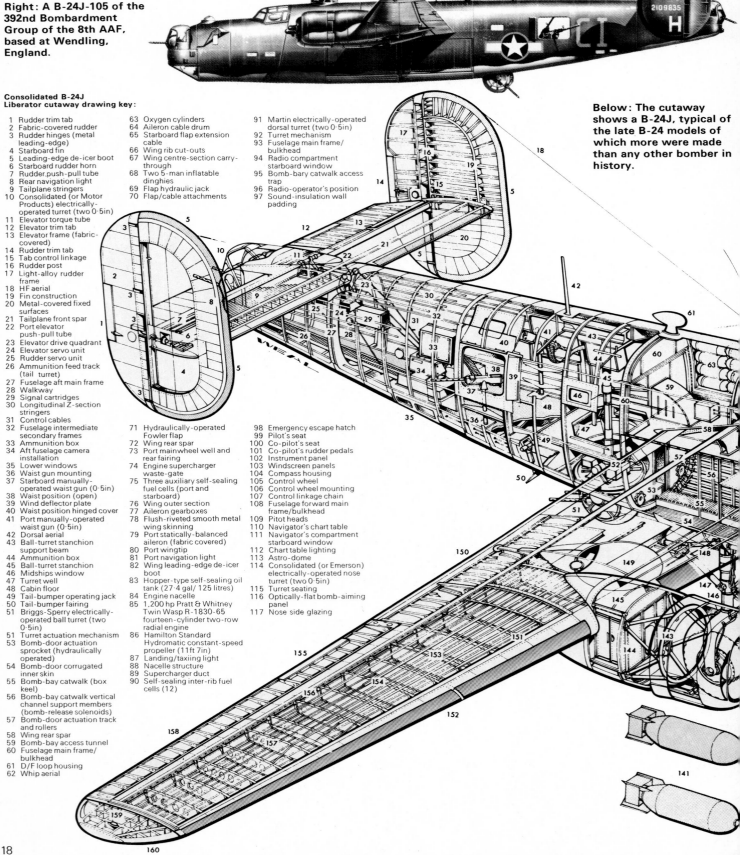

Below: The cutaway shows a B-24J, typical of the late B-24 models of which more were made than any other bomber in history.

1 Rudder trim tab
2 Fabric-covered rudder
3 Rudder hinges (metal leading-edge)
4 Starboard fin
5 Leading-edge de-icer boot
6 Starboard rudder horn
7 Rudder push-pull tube
8 Rear navigation light
9 Tailplane stringers
10 Consolidated (or Motor Products) electrically-operated turret (two 0·5in)
11 Elevator torque tube
12 Elevator trim tab
13 Elevator frame (fabric-covered)
14 Rudder trim tab
15 Tab control linkage
16 Rudder post
17 Light-alloy rudder frame
18 HF aerial
19 Fin construction
20 Metal-covered fixed surfaces
21 Tailplane front spar
22 Port elevator push-pull tube
23 Elevator drive quadrant
24 Elevator servo unit
25 Rudder servo unit
26 Ammunition feed track (tail turret)
27 Fuselage aft main frame
28 Walkway
29 Signal cartridges
30 Longitudinal Z-section stringers
31 Control cables
32 Fuselage intermediate secondary frames
33 Ammunition box
34 Aft fuselage camera installation
35 Lower windows
36 Waist gun mounting
37 Starboard manually-operated waist gun (0·5in)
38 Waist position (open)
39 Wind deflector plate
40 Waist position hinged cover
41 Port manually-operated waist gun (0·5in)
42 Dorsal aerial
43 Ball-turret stanchion support beam
44 Ammunition box
45 Ball-turret stanchion
46 Midships window
47 Turret well
48 Cabin floor
49 Tail-bumper operating jack
50 Tail-bumper fairing
51 Briggs-Sperry electrically-operated ball turret (two 0·5in)
51 Turret actuation mechanism
53 Bomb-door actuation sprocket (hydraulically operated)
54 Bomb-door corrugated inner skin
55 Bomb-bay catwalk (box keel)
56 Bomb-bay catwalk vertical channel support members (bomb-release solenoids)
57 Bomb-door actuation track and rollers
58 Wing rear spar
59 Bomb-bay access tunnel
60 Fuselage main frame/bulkhead
61 D/F loop housing
62 Whip aerial

63 Oxygen cylinders
64 Aileron cable drum
65 Starboard flap extension cable
66 Wing rib cut-outs
67 Wing centre-section carry-through
68 Two 5-man inflatable dinghies
69 Flap hydraulic jack
70 Flap/cable attachments
71 Hydraulically-operated Fowler flap
72 Wing rear spar
73 Port mainwheel well and rear fairing
74 Engine supercharger waste-gate
75 Three auxiliary self-sealing fuel cells (port and starboard)
76 Wing outer section
77 Aileron gearboxes
78 Flush-riveted smooth metal wing skinning
79 Port statically-balanced aileron (fabric covered)
80 Port wingtip
81 Port navigation light
82 Wing leading-edge de-icer boot
83 Hopper-type self-sealing oil tank (27·4 gal/125 litres)
84 Engine nacelle
85 1,200 hp Pratt & Whitney Twin Wasp R-1830-65 fourteen-cylinder two-row radial engine
86 Hamilton Standard Hydromatic constant-speed propeller (11ft 7in)
87 Landing/taxiing light
88 Nacelle structure
89 Supercharger duct
90 Self-sealing inter-rib fuel cells (12)

91 Martin electrically-operated dorsal turret (two 0·5in)
92 Turret mechanism
93 Fuselage main frame/bulkhead
94 Radio compartment starboard window
95 Bomb-bay catwalk access trap
96 Radio-operator's position
97 Sound-insulation wall padding
98 Emergency escape hatch
99 Pilot's seat
100 Co-pilot's seat
101 Co-pilot's rudder pedals
102 Instrument panel
103 Windscreen panels
104 Compass housing
105 Control wheel
106 Control wheel mounting
107 Control linkage chain
108 Fuselage forward main frame/bulkhead
109 Pitot heads
110 Navigator's chart table
111 Navigator's compartment starboard window
112 Chart table lighting
113 Astro-dome
114 Consolidated (or Emerson) electrically-operated nose turret (two 0·5in)
115 Turret seating
116 Optically-flat bomb-aiming panel
117 Nose side glazing

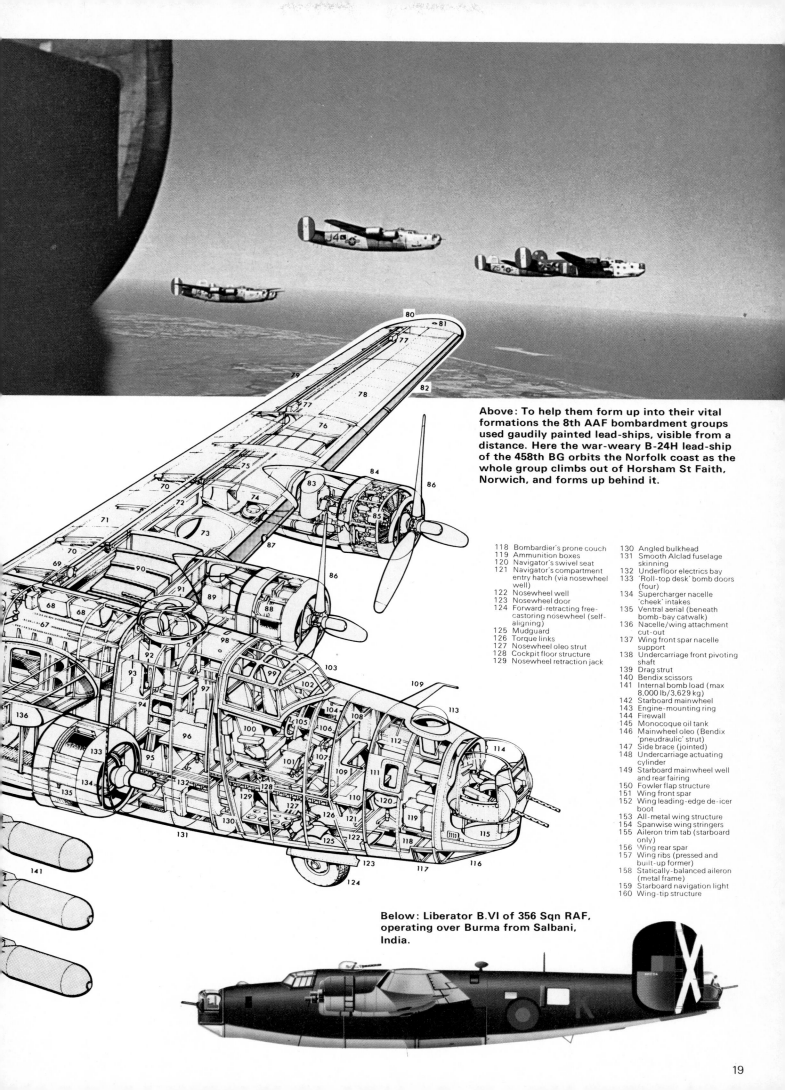

Above: To help them form up into their vital formations the 8th AAF bombardment groups used gaudily painted lead-ships, visible from a distance. Here the war-weary B-24H lead-ship of the 458th BG orbits the Norfolk coast as the whole group climbs out of Horsham St Faith, Norwich, and forms up behind it.

118 Bombardier's prone couch
119 Ammunition boxes
120 Navigator's swivel seat
121 Navigator's compartment entry hatch (via nosewheel well)
122 Nosewheel well
123 Nosewheel door
124 Forward-retracting free-castoring nosewheel (self-aligning)
125 Mudguard
126 Torque links
127 Nosewheel oleo strut
128 Cockpit floor structure
129 Nosewheel retraction jack

130 Angled bulkhead
131 Smooth Alclad fuselage skinning
132 Underfloor electrics bay
133 'Roll-top desk' bomb doors (four)
134 Supercharger nacelle 'cheek' intakes
135 Ventral aerial (beneath bomb-bay catwalk)
136 Nacelle/wing attachment cut-out
137 Wing front spar nacelle support
138 Undercarriage front pivoting shaft
139 Drag strut
140 Bendix scissors
141 Internal bomb load (max 8,000 lb/3,629 kg)
142 Starboard mainwheel
143 Engine-mounting ring
144 Firewall
145 Monocoque oil tank
146 Mainwheel oleo (Bendix 'pneudraulic' strut)
147 Side brace (jointed)
148 Undercarriage actuating cylinder
149 Starboard mainwheel well and rear fairing
150 Fowler flap structure
151 Wing front spar
152 Wing leading-edge de-icer boot
153 All-metal wing structure
154 Spanwise wing stringers
155 Aileron trim tab (starboard only)
156 Wing rear spar
157 Wing ribs (pressed and built-up former)
158 Statically-balanced aileron (metal frame)
159 Starboard navigation light
160 Wing-tip structure

Below: Liberator B.VI of 356 Sqn RAF, operating over Burma from Salbani, India.

Consolidated Vultee
Model 33 B-32 Dominator

XB-32, B-32 and TB-32

Origin: Consolidated Vultee Aircraft Corporation (Convair), Fort Worth, Texas; second-source production by Convair, San Diego.
Type: Long-range strategic bomber; (TB) crew trainer.
Engines: Four 2,300hp Wright R-3350-23 Duplex Cyclone 18-cylinder radials.
Dimensions: Span 135ft 0in (41·15m); length 83ft 1in (25·33m); height 32ft 9in (9·98m).
Weights: Empty 60,272lb (27,340kg); loaded 111,500lb (50,576kg); maximum 120,000lb (54,432kg).
Performance: Maximum speed 365mph (587km/h); service ceiling at normal loaded weight 35,000ft (10,670m); range (max bomb load) 800 miles (1287km), (max fuel) 3,800 miles (6115km).
Armament: (XB) two 20mm and 14 0·50in guns in seven remote-controlled turrets; (B) ten 0·50in in nose, two dorsal, ventral and tail turrets; max bomb load 20,000lb (9072kg) in tandem fuselage bays.
History: First flight (XB) 7 September 1942; service delivery (B) 1 November 1944.
User: USA (AAF).

Development: Ordered in September 1940, a month after the XB-29, the XB-32 was designed to the same Hemisphere Defense Weapon specification and followed similar advanced principles with pressurized cabins and remote-controlled turrets. Obviously related to the smaller B-24, the XB-32 had a slender wing passing above the capacious bomb bays, but the twin-wheel main gears folded into the large inner nacelles. There was a smoothly streamlined nose, like the XB-29, and twin fins. The second aircraft introduced a stepped pilot windscreen and the third a vast single fin like the final B-24 versions. Eventually the heavy and complex armament system was scrapped and replaced by simpler manned turrets, while in late 1943 the decision was taken to eliminate the troublesome pressurization and operate at 30,000ft or below. The B-32 was late and disappointing, though still a great performer. Large orders were placed at Fort Worth and San Diego, but only 115 had been delivered by VJ-day and a single squadron in the Marianas made two combat missions.

Right: It is a reflection on the development problems of the B-32 that roughly half the available photographs show aircraft lacking armament. This picture does depict a fully operational machine with a crew of eight including five gunners each in a powered turret. Propellers were 17ft Curtiss Electrics.

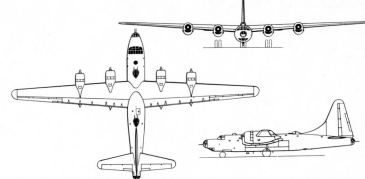

Above: Three-view of B-32 (TB-32 similar).

Consolidated Vultee
Model 28 PBY Catalina

PBY-1 to PBY-5A Catalina (data for -5)

Origin: Consolidated Vultee Aircraft Corporation; also made by Naval Aircraft Factory, Canadian Vickers, Boeing Canada, and Soviet Union (Taganrog).
Type: Maritime patrol flying boat with normal crew of seven.
Engines: Two 1,200hp Pratt & Whitney R-1830-92 Twin Wasp 14-cylinder two-row radials.
Dimensions: Span 104ft 0in (31·72m); length 63ft 11in (19·5m); height 18ft 10in (5·65m).
Weights: Empty 17,465lb (7974kg); loaded 34,000lb (15,436kg).
Performance: Maximum speed 196mph (314km/h); climb to 5,000ft (1525m) in 4min 30sec; service ceiling 18,200ft (5550m); range at 100mph (161km/h) 3,100 miles (4960km).
Armament: US Navy, typically one 0·30in or 0·50in Browning in nose, one 0·50in in each waist blister and one in "tunnel" in underside behind hull step; RAF typically six 0·303in Vickers K (sometimes Brownings) arranged one in nose, one in tunnel and pairs in blisters; wing racks for 2,000lb (907kg) of bombs and other stores.
History: First flight (XP3Y-1) 21 March 1935; first delivery (PBY-1) October 1936; (Model 28–5 Catalina) July 1939; final delivery, after December 1945.
Users: Australia, Brazil, Canada, Chile, Netherlands, New Zealand, Norway, Soviet Union, UK (RAF), US (AAF, Navy, Marines), Uruguay.

Development: Consolidated of Buffalo battled with Douglas of Santa Monica in 1933 to supply the US Navy with its first cantilever monoplane flying boat. Though the Douglas was good, its rival, designed by Isaac M. Laddon, was to be a classic aircraft and made in bigger numbers than any other flying boat before or since, by the new plant at San Diego. Its features included two 825hp Twin Wasps mounted close together on a wide clean wing, on the tips of which were to be found the retracted stabilising floats. The XP3Y-1, as it was called, clocked a speed of 184mph, which was high for a 1935 flying boat. The order for 60 was exceptional for those days, but

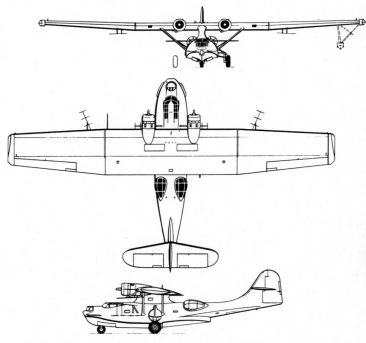

Above: Three-view of PBY-5A (Catalina IIA and III) with radar.

within a decade the total had topped 4,000. In 1938 three were bought by the Soviet Union, which urgently tooled up to build its own version, called GST, with M62 engines. In 1939 one was bought by the RAF, which soon placed large orders and called the boat Catalina, a name adopted in the USA in 1942. In December 1939 came the PBY-5A (OA-10) with retractable landing gear, which was named Canso by the RCAF. Many hundreds of both the boat and the amphibian were built by Canadian Vickers (as the PBV-1) and Boeing Canada (PB2B-1) and revised tall-fin

Consolidated Vultee PB4Y-2 Privateer

PB4Y-2 (P4Y-2) Privateer

Origin: Consolidated Vultee Aircraft Corporation.
Type: Maritime patrol bomber with normal crew of 11.
Engines: Four 1,200hp Pratt & Whitney R-1830-94 Twin Wasp 14-cylinder two-row radials.
Dimensions: Span 110ft 0in (33·5m); length 74ft 0in (22·6m); height 26ft 1in (7·9m).
Weights: Empty 41,000lb (18,600kg); loaded 65,000lb (29,484kg).
Performance: Maximum speed 247mph (399km/h); initial climb 800ft (244m)/min; service ceiling 19,500ft (5970m); range with maximum ordnance load 2,630 miles (4230km).
Armament: Consolidated nose and tail turrets, two Martin dorsal turrets and two Erco blister-type waist turrets each armed with two 0·50in Brownings; internal bomb bay similar to B-24 accommodating up to 6,000lb (2725kg) bombs, depth charges and other stores. In PB4Y-2B provision to launch and control two ASM-N-2 Bat air-to-surface missiles.
History: First flight (XPB4Y-2) 20 September 1943; first production delivery July 1944; final delivery September 1945.
Users: China, France, US (Navy).

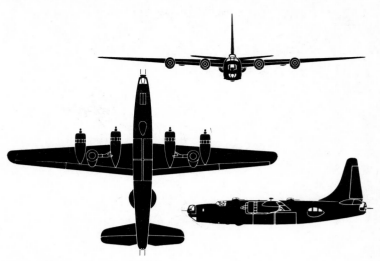

Above: Three-view of PB4Y-2 Privateer.

Development: In May 1943 the US Navy placed a contract with Convair (Consolidated Vultee Aircraft) for a long-range oversea patrol bomber derived from the B-24 Liberator. Three B-24Ds were taken off the San Diego line and largely rebuilt, with fuselages 7ft longer, with completely different interior arrangements, radically altered defensive armament and many airframe changes, such as hot-air de-icing and engine cowlings in the form of vertical ovals instead of flattened horizontal ones. The distinctive vertical tail was similar to that adopted on the final Liberator transport versions (C-87C, RY-3 and RAF C.IX) and much taller than that of the Liberator B-24N. The Navy bought a straight run of 739, of which 286 were delivered in 1944 and 453 in 1945. From the start performance was lower than that of Liberators of equal power because of the bigger and heavier airframe, extra equipment and emphasis on low-level missions. Over the ten years of service the Privateer — called P4Y from 1951 — grew more and more radar and secret countermeasures and finally made long electronic probing flights round (and probably over) the edges of the Soviet Union, at least one being shot down in the process. Over 80 served with the French Aéronavale and Chinese Nationalist Air Force.

Right: The resemblance to a B-24 is superficial; they were in fact totally different aircraft, apart from the basic wing.

Above: Depth-charge attack on a U-boat by an early RAF "Cat" in 1941. This was the year that a Catalina found the Bismarck.

Right: During World War II the PBY served all over the world. This busy mooring operation with the US Navy in 1942 probably took place in the Aleutians, though that is a mere guess from the scenery. Under the right wing are depth bombs.

versions were made at New Orleans (PBY-6A) and by the Naval Aircraft Factory at Philadelphia (PBN-1). The "Cat's" exploits are legion. One found the *Bismarck* in mid-Atlantic; one attacked a Japanese carrier in daylight after radioing: "Please inform next of kin"; in 1942 Patrol Squadron 12 started the Black Cat tradition of stealthy night devastation; and one had both ailerons ripped off by a storm but crossed the Atlantic and landed safely. Hundreds served in many countries for long after World War II.

Consolidated Vultee Model 29 PB2Y Coronado

PB2Y-1 to -5

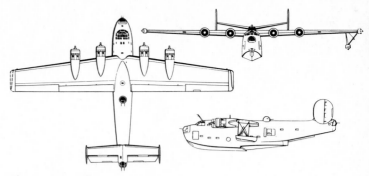

Origin: Consolidated Aircraft (Consolidated Vultee, or Convair, from March 1943), San Diego, Calif.
Type: Ocean patrol, transport and ambulance flying boat.
Engines: Four 1,200hp Pratt & Whitney R-1830 Twin Wasp 14-cylinder radials (see text).
Dimensions: Span (floats up) 115ft 0in (35·05m); length (all, within 4in) 79ft 3in (24·16m); height 27ft 6in (8·38m).
Weights: Empty (-3) 40,935lb (18,568kg), (-3R) about 33,000lb (14,970kg); maximum (all) 68,000lb (30,845kg).
Performance: Maximum speed (typical) 223mph (359km/h); econ cruise 141mph (227km/h); range with max weapons (-3) 1,370 miles (2204km), (-5) 1,640 miles (2640km); max range (-3) 2,370 miles (3813km), (-5) 3,900 miles (6275km).
Armament: (Except transports) eight 0·5in guns in three power turrets and two manual beam windows; offensive load of up to 8,000lb (3629kg) internal plus 4,000lb (1814kg) external, including torpedoes.
History: First flight 17 December 1937; service delivery 31 December 1940; final delivery October 1943.
Users: UK (RAF), US (Navy).

Development: Few aircraft have been more extensively modified than the XPB2Y-1 in 1937—39, and the production PB2Y-2 of 1940 was again totally

Above: Three-view of PB2Y-3.

different with a vast new hull which nevertheless did not stop it reaching 255mph. The main production run of 210 boats was designated PB2Y-3. The -3B served with RAF Transport Command, the -3R was stripped of military gear and had low-rated R-1830-92 engines giving better low-level performance carrying 44 passengers or 16,000lb cargo, the -5 had more than 60 per cent more fuel and -92 engines, and the -5H was an unarmed ambulance. The Coronado was trusty but rather sluggish, and often needed the takeoff rockets which it pioneered. Most combat-equipped -3 and -5 had ASV radar above the flight deck.

Right: A standard PB2Y-3. Many were converted into -3R transport or -5 radar platforms with extra fuel and low-blown engines.

Curtiss Hawk 75 (P-36 Mohawk), 81 (P-40 Tomahawk), and 87 (P-40 Warhawk, Kittyhawk)

A: Hawk 75A, P-36A, Mohawk IV
B: Hawk 81A, P-40C, Tomahawk IIB
C: Hawk 87D, P-40F, Kittyhawk II
D: Hawk 87M, P-40N, Kittyhawk IV

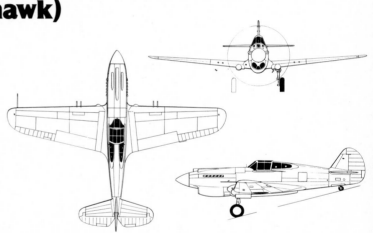

Origin: Curtiss-Wright Corporation.
Type: (A) single-seat fighter, (B) single-seat fighter, reconnaissance and ground attack; (C, D) single-seat fighter bomber.
Engine: (A) P-36A, 1,050hp Pratt & Whitney R-1830-13 Twin Wasp 14-cylinder two-row radial; Hawk 75A and Mohawk, 1,200hp Wright GR-1820-G205A Cyclone nine-cylinder radial; (B) 1,040hp Allison V-1710-33 vee-12 liquid-cooled; (C) 1,300hp Packard V-1650-1 (R-R Merlin) vee-12 liquid-cooled; (D) 1,200hp Allison V-1710-81, -99 or -115 vee-12 liquid-cooled.
Dimensions: Span 37ft 3½in (11·36m); length (A) 28ft 7in (8·7m), (B) 31ft 8½in (9·7m); (C) 31ft 2in (9·55m) or 33ft 4in (10·14m); (D) 33ft 4in (10·14m); height (A) 9ft 6in (2·89m), (B, C, D) 12ft 4in (3·75m).
Weights: Empty (A) 4,541lb (2060kg), (B) 5,812lb (2636kg), (C) 6,550lb (2974kg), (D) 6,700lb (3039kg); loaded (A) 6,662lb (3020kg), (B) 7,459lb (3393kg), (C) 8,720lb (3960kg), (D) 11,400lb (5008kg).
Performance: Maximum speed (A) 303mph (488km/h), (B) 345mph (555km/h), (C) 364mph (582km/h), (D) 343mph (552km/h); initial climb (A) 2,500ft (762m)/min, (B) 2,650ft (807m)/min, (C) 2,400ft (732m)/min, (D) 2,120ft (646m)/min; service ceiling (all) about 30,000ft (9144m); range on internal fuel (A) 680 miles (1,100km), (B) 730 miles (1175km), (C) 610 miles (976km), (D) 750 miles (1207km).

Above: Three-view of P-40C (Tomahawk similar).

Right: The middle-vintage Kittyhawks, roughly equivalent to the P-40D to N, were the most important fighter-bombers of the British Commonwealth air forces in the period from Alamein (October 1942) to the end of the war in northern Italy. Over 3,000 were in use, two of them being these Kittyhawk IIIs seen returning from a bombing mission in North Africa in early 1943. The ground-guidance "erk" had a rough ride.

Left: The Hawk 75C-1, equivalent to a P-36C or Mohawk, wrote a glorious chapter in Armée de l'Air service in 1939-40. Unlike many French programmes, the Hawk was delivered on time, and its crews were trained and capable in the nation's hour of need (but it had a hard time against the Bf 109E).

Left: This Tomahawk (British P-40C) is seen in the markings of No 349 (Belgian) Sqn, RAF, at Ikeja, West Africa, in early 1943.

Armament: (A) P-36A, one 0·50in and one 0·30in Brownings above engine; P-36C, as P-36A with two 0·30in in wings; Hawk 75A/Mohawk IV, six 0·303in (four in wings); (B) six 0·303in (four in wings); (C, D) six 0·50in in wings with 281 rounds per gun (early P-40N, only four); bomb load (A) underwing racks for total of 400lb (181kg); (B) nil; (C) one 500lb on centreline and 250lb (113kg) under each wing; (D) 500 or 600lb (272kg) on centreline and 500lb under each wing.

History: First flight (Model 75 prototype) May 1935; (first Y1P-36) January 1937; (first production P-36A) April 1938; (XP-40) October 1938; (P-40) January 1940; (P-40D) 1941; (P-40F) 1941; (P-40N) 1943; final delivery (P-40N-40 and P-40R) December 1944.

Users: Argentina, Australia, Belgium, Bolivia, Brazil, Canada, China,

Colombia, Egypt, Finland, France, Iraq, Italy (CB), Netherlands, New Zealand, Norway, Peru, Portugal, S. Africa, Soviet Union, Turkey, UK (RAF), US (AAC/AAF).

Development: In November 1934 Curtiss began the design of a completely new "Hawk" fighter with cantilever monoplane wing, backwards retracting landing gear (the wheels turning 90° to lie inside the wing) and all-metal stressed-skin construction. After being tested by the Army Air Corps this design was put into production as the P-36A, marking a major advance in speed though not in firepower. Successive types of P-36 and its export counterpart, the Hawk 75A, had different engines and additional guns and

▶

▶ the Hawk 75A was bought in large numbers by many countries and made under licence in several. Biggest customer was the French Armée de l'Air, which began to receive the H75A in March 1939. Five groups — GC I/4, II/4, I/5, II/5 and III/2 — wrote a glorious chapter over France in May 1940, invariably outnumbered and usually outperformed, but destroying 311 of the Luftwaffe, more than the total H75A strength when France fell. The rest of the French orders were supplied to the RAF as Mohawks, serving mainly on the Burma front.

More than 1,300 radial-engined models were delivered, but the real story began with the decision in July 1937 to build the P-40, with the liquid-cooled Allison engine. This was a novel and untried engine in a land where aircraft engines had become universally air-cooled, and teething troubles were long and severe. Eventually, towards the end of 1940, the P-40B and RAF Tomahawk I were cleared for combat duty and the process of development began. The rest of the aircraft was almost unchanged and in comparison with the Bf109 or Spitfire the early P-40 showed up badly, except in the twin attributes of manoeuvrability and strong construction. Eventually the RAF, RAAF and SAAF took 885 of three marks of Tomahawk, used as low-level army co-operation machines in Britain and as ground

Left: Field maintenance on a P-40F Warhawk, probably in Tunisia or Sicily. This model had the Packard V-1650 (Merlin) with updraught carburettor (hence no duct above the cowling).

Below: The cutaway depicts the Hawk 75A-2 as used by the Armée de l'Air in 1940 and by Commonwealth air forces as various marks of Mohawk. The A-2 model, first ordered in January 1939, had two extra wing guns. Not all radial Hawks had the Twin Wasp; many used the single-row Cyclone.

Curtis Hawk 75A-2 cutaway drawing key:

1 Curtiss Electric hub
2 Forged light-alloy blades
3 Ports for fuselage-mounted 7·5 mm FN-Browning Mle 38 machine guns
4 Pratt & Whitney R-1830-SC3-G Twin Wasp 14-cylinder two-row radial engine
5 Machine gun barrel extension collars
6 Air-cooling duct
7 Exhaust outlet
8 Engine bearers
9 Cooling gills
10 Oil tank
11 Secondary ring-and-bead sight
12 Machine gun breeches
13 Cooling louvres
14 Forward fuel tank (35 Imp gal/159 litres capacity)
15 Rudder pedals
16 Pilot's seat (accommodating Lemercier back-type parachute)
17 Control column
18 Baille-Lemaire gunsight
19 Aft-sliding canopy
20 Pilot's head and back armour
21 Fuel filler cap
22 Canopy track
23 Overload fuel tank (48 Imp gal/217 litres capacity)
24 Elevator trim cable
25 Handhold
26 Fuselage construction
27 Rear-view cutout
28 Aerial mast
29 Radio aerial
30 Stressed-skin fuselage
31 Light-alloy fin
32 Formation lights
33 Rudder hinge
34 Fabric-covered rudder
35 Fabric-covered elevator
36 Tailplane
37 Tailwheel door
38 Retractable tailwheel
39 Tailwheel oleo and retraction jack
40 Lift point
41 Rudder trim cable
42 Elevator cables
43 Servicing and access panel
44 Radio-Industrie 537 R/T equipment
45 Batteries
46 Wing fillet
47 Aft underfloor fuel tank (25 Imp gal/113 litres capacity)
48 Forward underfloor fuel tank (27 Imp gal/125 litres capacity)
49 Bevel drive
50 Bevel/oleo leg rotating point
51 Undercarriage fairing
52 Undercarriage fairing door
53 Mainwheel
54 Two 7·5 mm FN-Browning Mle 38 machine guns
55 Mainwheel leg
56 Retraction actuator rod
57 Wheel well
58 Split flaps
59 Wing gun breeches
60 Stressed wing skinning
61 Ammunition feed trays
62 Aileron trim tab
63 Fabric-covered aileron
64 Wing construction
65 Port navigation lamps (upper and lower)
66 Pitot tube

attack fighters in North Africa. Many hundreds of other P-40Bs and Cs were supplied to the US Army, Soviet Union, China and Turkey.

With the P-40D a new series of Allison engines allowed the nose to be shortened and the radiator was deepened, changing the appearance of the aircraft. The fuselage guns were finally thrown out and the standard armament became the much better one of six ''fifties'' in the wings. The RAF had ordered 560 of the improved fighters in 1940, and they were called Kittyhawk I. When the US Army bought it the name Warhawk was given to subsequent P-40 versions. The Merlin engine went into production in the USA in 1941 and gave rise to the P-40F; none of the 1,311 Merlin P-40s reached the RAF, most going to the Soviet Union, US Army and Free French. Most Fs introduced a longer fuselage to improve directional stability. Subsequent models had a dorsal fin as well and reverted to the Allison engine. Great efforts were made to reduce weight and improve performance, because the whole family was fundamentally outclassed by the other front-line fighters on both sides; but, predictably, weight kept rising. It reached its peak in the capable and well-equipped P-40N, of which no fewer than 4,219 were built. Some of the early Ns had all the weight-savings and could reach 378mph (608km/h), but they were exceptions. Altogether deliveries of P-40 versions to the US government amounted to 13,738. Though it was foolhardy to tangle with a crack enemy fighter in close combat the Hawk family were tough, nimble and extremely useful weapons, especially in close support of armies.

Above: Air-to-air of a middle-vintage P-40E (modified to K standard with anti-swing dorsal fin) with the definitive armament of ''six fifties'', two more than on the D. The red-outlined insignia soon gave way to dark blue.

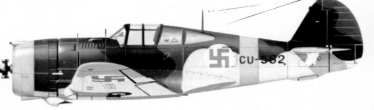

Above: Finland received 36 Hawks of various sub-types captured by the Germans and overhauled by them. This A-3 of 32 Sqn, Suulajärvi, has an R-1830 Twin Wasp (yellow band denotes Soviet front).

Above: Kittyhawk III (P-40K) of the RNZAF serving on Guadalcanal in late 1942.

Above: An early bird, a P-40C of the US Army Air Corps 77th Fighter Sqn, 20th Pursuit Group, at Hamilton Field in 1941.

Above: Another long-fuselage Kittyhawk III, this time serving with 250 Sqn of the RAF in southern Italy in 1943-44.

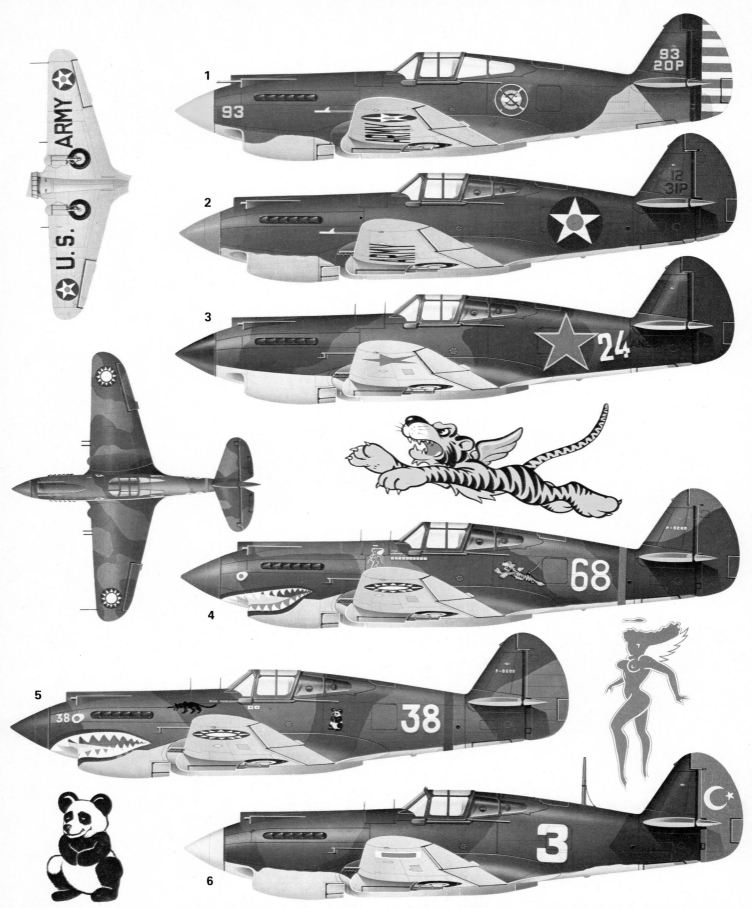

Above: Replacing the Hawk 75's air-cooled radial with a liquid-cooled Allison V-1710 engine produced the Hawk 81A, first flown in prototype form as the XP-40 in October 1940. Subsequent production models included the USAAF P-40B and C, the RAF Tomahawk I, IIA and IIB, and 100 Hawk 81A-1, -2 and -3 supplied to the American Volunteer Group in China; various models were supplied to several other countries.

1: P-40 in service with the 55th Squadron, 20th Pursuit Group, at Marsh Field, California, in 1941; underside markings are shown alongside;

2: P-40C of the 39th Squadron, 31st Pursuit group, Selfridge Field, in 1941.

3: Tomahawk IIB serving with the 154 IAP (Fighter Aviation Regiment), Red Banner Baltic Fleet Air Force, in the Leningrad area in 1942.

4: Hawk 81A-2 of the 3rd Squadron, AVG, based at Kunming, China, in the spring of 1942. Also shown are the upper surfaces, the AVG's "Flying Tigers" emblem, and the squadron's "Hell's Angels" emblem.

5: Hawk 81A-2 flown by Henry Geselbracht, 2nd Squadron, AVG, at Toungoo in February 1942, along with the aircraft's "Panda Bear" emblem.

6: A Tomahawk IIB in Turkish service in 1942.

26

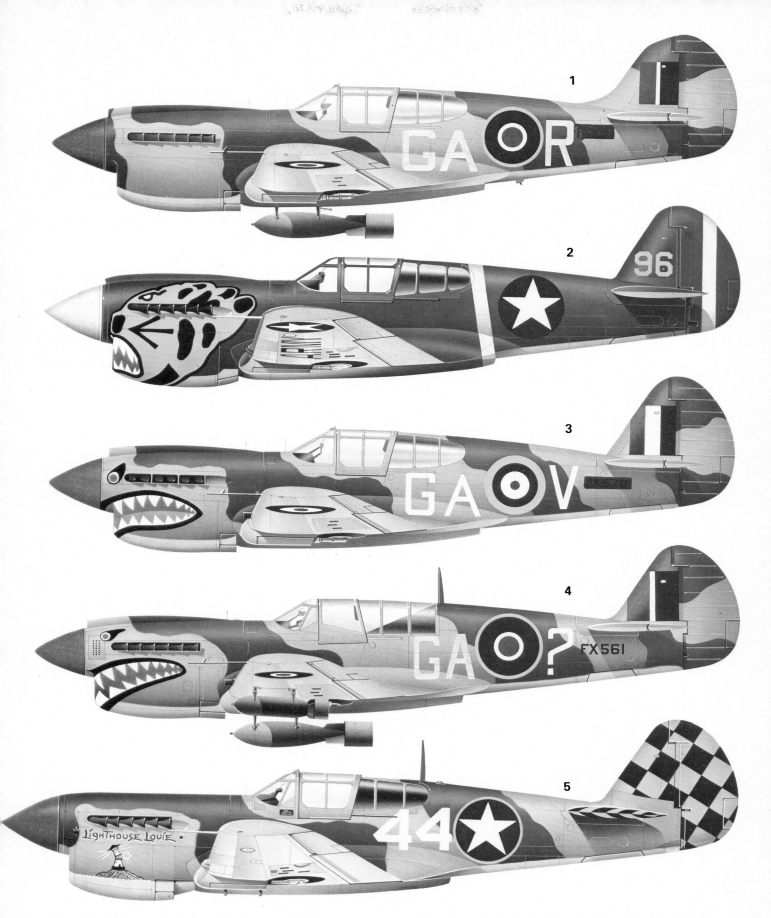

Above: The Hawk 87 series used various liquid-cooled engines in a redesigned nose: USAAF P-40D and subsequent models were named Warhawk, while in the RAF they were known as Kittyhawks. More than 11,800 were built, with the standard armament of six wing-mounted 0·50in machine guns, and production did not end until November 1944, but despite the more powerful engines used in the later models performance remained inferior in several areas to that of other front-line fighters.

1: Kittyhawk III serving with 112 Squadron, 239 Wing, RAF, based at Cutella, Italy, in 1944.

2: P-40E Warhawk serving with the 11th Squadron, 343rd Fighter Group, USAAF, in the Aleutians in 1942.

3: Kittyhawk I flown by Flying Officer Neville Duke of 112 Squadron, based at LG 91, south of Alexandria, in September 1942.

4: Another 112 Squadron aircraft, this time a Kittyhawk IV, also based at Cutella early in 1944.

5: P-40L-5 Warhawk flown by Lt Col G. H. Austin, serving with HQ Flight, 325th Fighter Group, based in Tunisia, in 1943.

Curtiss C-46 Commando

C-46A, D, E and F and R5C

Origin: Curtiss-Wright Corporation, Buffalo, NY; production at St Louis, Mo, and Louisville, Ky.
Type: Troop and cargo transport.
Engines: (A, D) two 2,000hp Pratt & Whitney R-2800-51 Double Wasp 18-cylinder radials, (E, F) 2,200hp R-2800-75.
Dimensions: Span 108ft 1in (32·92m); length 76ft 4in (23·27m); height 21ft 9in (6·63m).
Weights: Empty (A) 29,483lb (13,373kg); maximum (A) 50,000lb (22,680 kg).
Performance: Cruising speed (67 per cent) 227mph (365km/h), (econ) 193mph (31·1km/h); max range (no fuselage tanks) 1,600 miles (2575km), (max payload) 890 miles (1432km).
History: First flight 26 March 1940; service delivery (C-46) October 1941; final delivery 1945.
Users: (WWII) UK (BOAC), US (AAF, Navy).

Development: In 1936 Curtiss-Wright planned an exceptionally large and capable twin-engined airliner, of modern stressed-skin type, to try to recover its airline sales that had been swept away by the new monoplanes from Boeing, Lockheed and Douglas. In 1940 the CW-20 impressed not only airlines but also the US Army, and it was totally redesigned as a military transport. The sumptuous pressurized fuselage was replaced by an unpressurized one with large doors and strong floor; twin fins became one, the R-2600 engines became more powerful R-2800s and the whole machine was tailored to quick production and troublefree service. By 1945 about 3,330 of these extremely useful aircraft had been delivered, almost all as

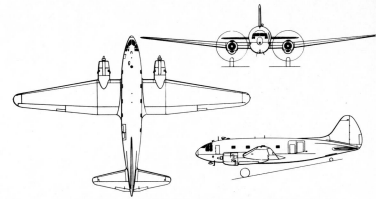

Above: Three-view of C-46A (all models generally similar).

various C-46 models but 160 being Navy R5C-1. Carrying up to 40 passengers or about 12,000lb (5440kg) of cargo, they were the mainliners of the "Hump" airlift to China, and by late 1944 were also numerous in Europe, taking part in the Rhine crossing. Though Curtiss never did achieve the civil sales they sought, the ex-wartime C-46 was destined to play a major role in outback nations right up to the present day, about 140 still being in daily use in Latin America.

Right: One of the first C-46As to be delivered to the US Army in 1941. Later blocks were unpainted and had numerous minor improvements. The RAF used a converted bomber, the Warwick, as a transport with half the capacity but the same engines.

Curtiss SB2C/A-25 Helldiver

SB2C-1 to -5 (data for -1)

Origin: Curtiss-Wright Corporation; also built by Fairchild and Canadian Car & Foundry (CanCar).
Type: Two-seat carrier-based dive bomber.
Engine: 1,700hp Wright R-2600-8 Cyclone 14-cylinder two-row radial.
Dimensions: Span 49ft 9in (15·2m); length 36ft 8in (11·2m); height 16ft 11in (5·1m).
Weights: Empty 11,000lb (4990kg); loaded 16,607lb (7550kg).
Performance: Maximum speed 281mph (452km/h); service ceiling 24,700ft (7530m); range 1,110 miles (1786km).
Armament: Two 20mm or four 0·50in guns in wings and two 0·30in or one 0·50in in rear cockpit; provision for 1,000lb (454kg) bomb load internally (later versions added wing racks).
History: First flight (XSB2C-1) 18 December 1940; (production SB2C-1) June 1942; termination of production 1945.
Users: US (AAF, Navy, Marines).

Development: During World War II, by far the most successful Allied dive bomber was the Helldiver, which perpetuated a Curtiss trade-name established with a biplane dive bomber used by the US Navy as the SBC series and, briefly, by the RAF as the Cleveland. The new monoplane was a totally different design, with very powerful engine, large folding wing and internal bomb bay. Yet development took a long time, partly because the prototype crashed but mainly because the US services asked for 880 further major design changes after the SB2C-1 had been frozen for production in November 1941. This was partly for Army/Navy/Marine Corps standardization, the Army/Marines aircraft being called A-25 Shrike or SB2C-1A. Eventually production rolled ahead at Curtiss, at Fairchild (who built SBFs) and Canadian Car & Foundry (who made SBWs). Altogether 7,200 Helldivers were delivered, roughly equally divided between the -1, -3, -4 and -5 subtypes. The -2 was a twin-float seaplane. From Rabaul in November 1943 Helldivers fought hard and effectively in every major action of the Pacific war.

Right: This Helldiver sub-type about to recover aboard its flat-top is probably a -3 (SB2C-3, SBF-3 or SBW-3). Total -3 production was 1,112, compared with 978 -1, 2,045 -4 and 970 -5.

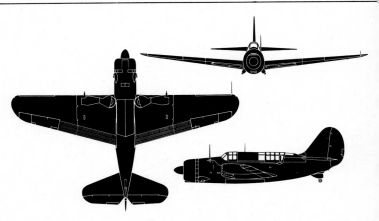

Above: Three-view of SB2C-4 (most sub-types generally similar).

Left: This SB2C-1 was assigned to squadron VB-8 (heavier-than-air bomber, No 8) of the US Navy, embarked aboard carriers in the Saipan campaign (indeed, it saw action in most Pacific battles).

Right: The 20mm cannon muzzle immediately outboard of the landing-gear leg proclaims this Helldiver to be a -3 or later model. On land airfields the high-pressure tyres and hard-rubber tailwheel could cause problems; this single engined aircraft had a gross weight similar to that of many twins.

Douglas DB-7 family A-20, Boston, Havoc

A-20, Boston, Havoc, BD-2, F-3 and P-70

Origin: Douglas Aircraft Company; (Boston IIIA, Boeing Airplane Company).

Type: Two-seat fighter and intruder, three-seat bomber or two-seat reconnaissance aircraft.

Engines: Early DB-7 versions (Boston I, II, Havoc II) two 1,200hp Pratt & Whitney R-1830-S3C4-G Twin Wasp 14-cylinder two-row radials; all later versions, two 1,500, 1,600 or 1,700hp Wright GR-2600-A5B, -11, -23 or -29 Double Cyclone 14-cylinder two-row radials.

Dimensions: Span 61ft 4in (18·69m); length varied from 45ft 11in to 48ft 10in (A-20G, 48ft 4in, 14·74m); height 17ft 7in (5·36m).

Weights: Early Boston/Havoc, typically empty 11,400lb (5171kg), loaded 16,700lb (7574kg); (A-20G, typical of main production) empty 12,950lb (5874kg), loaded 27,200lb (12,340kg).

Performance: Maximum speed, slowest early versions 295mph (475km/h); fastest versions 351mph (565km/h); (A-20G) 342mph (549km/h); initial climb 1,200–2,000ft (366–610m)/min; service ceiling typically 25,300ft (7720m); range with maximum weapon load typically 1,000 miles (1,610km).

Armament: (Havoc I), eight 0·303in Brownings in nose, one 0·303in Vickers K manually aimed in rear cockpit; (Havoc II) twelve 0·303in in nose, (Havoc intruder), four 0·303in in nose, one Vickers K, and 1,000lb (454kg) bomb load; (A-20B) two fixed 0·5in Brownings on sides of nose, one 0·5in manually aimed dorsal, one 0·30in manually aimed ventral, 2,000lb (907kg) bomb load; (Boston III bomber) four fixed 0·303in on sides of nose, twin manually aimed 0·303in dorsal, twin manually aimed 0·303in ventral, 2,000lb (907kg) bomb load; (Boston III intruder) belly tray of four 20mm Hispano cannon, 2,000lb (907kg) bomb load; (A-20G) four 20mm and two 0·5in or six 0·5in in nose, dorsal turret with two 0·5in, manually aimed 0·5in ventral, 4,000lb (1814kg) bomb load. Many other schemes, early A-20s having fixed rearward firing 0·30in in each nacelle.

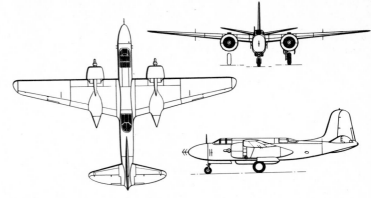

Above: Three-view of P-70 with four M-2 cannon and AI.IV radar.

History: First flight (Douglas 7B) 26 October 1938; (production DB-7) 17 August 1939; service delivery (France) 2 January 1940; termination of production September 1944.

Users: Australia, Brazil, Canada, France, Netherlands, New Zealand, South Africa, Soviet Union, UK (RAF), US (AAC/AAF, Navy).

Development: Designed by Jack Northrop and Ed Heinemann, the DB-7 family was one of the great combat aircraft of all time. Originally planned to meet a US Army Air Corps attack specification of 1938, it was dramatically altered and given more powerful Twin Wasp engines and a nosewheel-type landing gear (for the first time in a military aircraft). In February 1939 the French government ordered 100 of a further modified type, with deeper but narrower fuselage and other gross changes. This model, the DB-7, went into production at El Segundo and Santa Monica, with 1,764lb (800kg) bomb load and armament of six 7·5mm MAC 1934 machine guns. Delivery took place via Casablanca and about 100 reached the Armée de l'Air, beginning operations on 31 May 1940. Much faster than other bombers, the DB-7 was judged "hot", because it was a modern aircraft in an environment of small unpaved airfields and because it was very different, and more complex, than contemporary European machines. One unusual feature was the emergency control column in the rear gunner's cockpit for use if the pilot should be killed. A few DB-7s escaped to Britain, where most of the French order was diverted (increased to 270 by 1940), and over 100 were converted at Burtonwood, Lancs, into Havoc night fighters. Many Havocs had 2,700-million candlepower "Turbinlites" in the nose for finding enemy raiders by night, while 93 Sqn towed Long Aerial Mine charges on steel cables. In February 1942 the RAF began operations with the much more powerful Boston III; making daring daylight low-level raids over Europe, while production of the first US Army A-20s got into its stride. By far the most important model was the A-20G, with heavier bomb load, dorsal turret and devastating nose armament. Among many other important US Army versions were the P-70 night fighters and the transparent-nosed A-20J and K, often used as bombing lead ships by the 9th and 15th Air Forces (respectively in Northwest Europe and Italy). The RAF counterparts of the J and K were the Boston IV and V, of the 2nd Tactical Air Force and Desert AF (Italy). Total production of this hard-hitting aircraft was 7,385, of which 3,125 were supplied freely to the Soviet Union.

Above: There were many intruder sub-types. This is an early P-70A with the nose armament later fitted to some A-20G attack bombers: four 20mm M-2 cannon. This example has no radar.

Below: A-20G attack bomber, in 9th Air Force insignia, with twin-0·5in turret.

Below: Boston III with painted-over nose, used on intruder and close-support missions by 22 Sqn RAAF in south-west Pacific.

Below: This Havoc I, of 23 Sqn, RAF, based at Ford, Sussex, in 1940, is the oldest aircraft depicted on this spread. Visually distinguished by having the original smaller vertical tail, it has the lower-powered Twin Wasp engines without the night flame-suppressing exhaust later developed. This was a bomber-intruder; other Havoc Is had cannon instead.

Below: A Boston IIIA of 88 Sqn, RAF, operating with 2nd TAF in France, 1944.

Below: Skip-bombing by 5th Air Force A-20s on a Japanese freighter.

Above: A squadron of Boston III attack bombers of the RAF over North Africa.

Below: The A-20J and K were fitted with glazed noses as bombardier lead-ships.

Douglas A-26 Invader

A-26 (later B-26) and JD-1 Invader; rebuilt as B-26K, redesignated A-26A

Origin: Douglas Aircraft Company; (post-war B-26K) On Mark Engineering.
Type: Three-seat attack bomber; FA-26 reconnaissance, JD target tug.
Engines: Two 2,000hp Pratt & Whitney R-2800-27, -71 or -79 Double Wasp 18-cylinder two-row radials; On Mark B-26K, 2,500hp R-2800-103W.
Dimensions: Span 70ft (21·34m) (B-26K, 75ft, 22·86m, over tip tanks); length 50ft (15·24m); height 18ft 6in (5·64m).
Weights: Empty, typically 22,370lb (10,145kg); loaded, originally 27,000lb (12,247kg) with 32,000lb (14,515kg) maximum overload, later increased to 35,000lb (15,876kg) with 38,500lb (17,460kg) maximum overload.
Performance: Maximum speed 355mph (571km/h); initial climb 2,000ft (610m)/min; service ceiling 22,100ft (6736m); range with maximum bomb load 1,400 miles (2253km).
Armament: (A-26B) ten 0·5in Brownings, six fixed in nose and two each in dorsal and ventral turrets; internal bomb load of 4,000lb (1814kg), later supplemented by underwing load of up to 2,000lb (907kg); (A-26C) similar but only two 0·5in in nose; (B-26K, A-26A) various nose configurations with up to eight 0·5in or four 20mm, plus six 0·30in guns in wings and total ordnance load of 8,000lb (3629kg) in bomb bay and on eight outer-wing pylons.
History: First flight (XA-26) 10 July 1942; service delivery December 1943; final delivery 2 January 1946; first flight of B-26K, February 1963.
Users: US (AAF, Navy).

Development: The Douglas Invader has a unique history. It was one of very few aircraft to be entirely conceived, designed, developed, produced in quantity and used in large numbers all during World War II. The whole programme was terminated after VJ-Day and anyone might have judged the aircraft finished. With new jets under development, Douglas made no effort to retain any design team on Invader development, neither did the Army Air Force show any interest. Yet this aircraft proved to be of vital importance in the Korean war and again in Vietnam and, by 1963, was urgently being manufactured for arduous front-line service. Some were in combat units 33 years after they were first delivered, a record no other kind of aircraft can equal. The design was prepared by Ed Heinemann at El Segundo as a natural successor to the DB-7 family, using the powerful new R-2800 engine. The Army Air Corps ordered three prototypes in May 1941, one with 75mm gun, one with four 20mm forward-firing cannon and four 0·5in guns in an upper turret, with radar nose, and the third as an attack bomber with optical sighting station in the nose and two defensive turrets. In the event it was the bomber that was bought first, designated A-26B. Much faster than other tactical bombers with the exception of the Mosquito, it was 700lb lighter than estimate, and capable of carrying twice the specified bomb load. It was the first bomber to use a NACA laminar-flow airfoil, double-slotted flaps and remote-control turrets (also a feature of the B-29). Combat missions with the 9th AF began on 19 November 1944 and these aircraft dropped over 18,000 tons of bombs on European targets. A total of 1,355 A-26Bs were delivered, the last 535 having -79 engines boosted by water injection. The A-26C, in service in January 1945, had a transparent nose, lead-ship navigational equipment and was often fitted with H_2S panoramic radar; production of this model was 1,091. In 1948 the B-26 Marauder was retired from service and the Invaders were redesignated B-26. Over 450 were used in Korea, and in Vietnam these fine

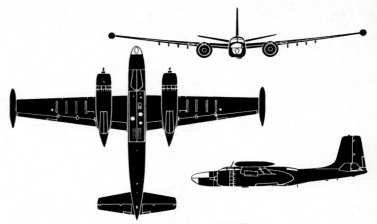

aircraft were one of the most favoured platforms for night attack on the Ho Chi Minh trail and in other interdiction areas. Though top speed was depressed to about 350mph, the A-26A (as the rebuilt B-26K was called) could carry up to 11,000lb (4990kg) of armament and deliver it accurately and, with 2 hr over target, over a wide radius. In 1977 six air forces retained Invader squadrons.

Above: Just over 1,000 of these glazed-nose A-26C Invaders were delivered, with a bombardier and two 0·5in guns in the glazed nose for visual bombing at all levels and lead-ship duties with formations of "solid-nose" A-26B Invaders.

Below: The A-26B was the chief model used in both the European and Pacific theatres in World War II. The devastating nose armament could be augmented by locking the remote-control upper turret to fire dead ahead. The A-26 suffered the lowest loss rate of any bomber in the European theatre.

Douglas B-18 Bolo, Digby

B-18, B-18A Bolo and Digby I

Origin: Douglas Aircraft Company.
Type: Heavy bomber (later maritime patrol) aircraft, with normal crew of six.
Engines: Two 930hp Wright R-1820-45 or -53 Cyclone nine-cylinder radials.
Dimensions: Span 89ft 0in (27·3m); length 57ft 10in (17·63m); height 15ft 2in (4·62m).
Weights: Empty 19,700lb (8936kg); loaded 27,673lb (12,550kg).
Performance: Maximum speed 215mph (349km/h); service ceiling 23,900ft (7285m); range with maximum bomb load 1,180 miles (1900km).
Armament: Normally one 0·30in Browning machine gun in nose, dorsal and retractable ventral positions, all aimed manually; internal bomb load of up to 4,000lb (1814kg).
History: First flight (DB-1) October 1935; service delivery (B-18) 1937; (B-18A) 1939.
Users: Brazil, Canada, US (AAC/AAF).

Development: In 1934 the United States Army issued a requirement for a new bomber to replace the Martin B-10. Martin entered an improved B-10, Boeing the four-engined Model 299 and Douglas the DB-1 (Douglas Bomber 1). It was the last-named which won and nobody at the time expected that, whereas the Douglas would have a short career and soon be forgotten, the controversial Boeing giant would become perhaps the most famous bomber in history. Douglas were awarded an immediate contract for the unprecedented number (since 1918, at least) of 133 aircraft, designated B-18. Based on the DC-2 transport, the B-18 had a fat body bulged under the wing to accommodate an internal bomb bay. Orders were later placed for a further 217 modified aircraft designated B-18A, plus a

Above: A brave pre-war sight, a squadron of B-18 heavy bombers captured in one of the first air-to-air colour photographs.

further 20 for the Royal Canadian Air Force called Digby (after the British bomber airfield). In 1937–40 this family was the most important heavy warplane in North America, but after that it faded rapidly. No big orders were placed by France or Britain, as was the case with all the newer American bombers, and the B-17 gradually replaced the B-18 in US Army bombardment squadrons. In 1941 122 B-18As were converted as anti-submarine patrol aircraft, with a large nose radome and the first MAD installation projecting behind the tail, for use in the Caribbean and off the east coast of the United States. The Digbys were also used for maritime duties until 1943. A few B-18s were later converted for use as business aircraft and several even remain in various types of civilian use.

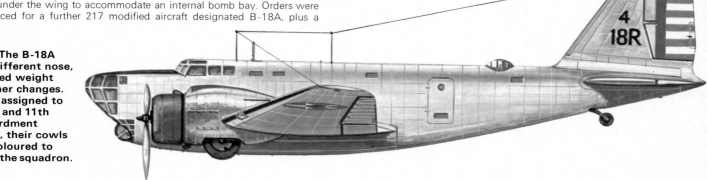

Right: The B-18A had a different nose, increased weight and other changes. Mainly assigned to the 5th and 11th Bombardment Groups, their cowls were coloured to denote the squadron.

Douglas DC-4 C-54 Skymaster

C-54A to J, R5D-1 to -6

Origin: Douglas Aircraft Company, Santa Monica.
Type: Strategic transport.
Engines: Four 1,350hp Pratt & Whitney R-2000-7 Twin Wasp 14-cylinder radials, (from late batches C-54D/R5D-3) R-2000-11, better altitude performance.
Dimensions: Span 117ft 6in (35·81m); length 93ft 11in (28·63m); height 27ft 6¼in (8·39m).
Weights: Empty (B) 38,200lb (17,328kg); maximum (B) 73,000lb (33,113kg).
Performance: Max cruise at optimum height 239mph (385km/h); max range with max useful load 1,500 miles (2414km); max range with max fuel 3,900 miles (6276km) at 190mph (306km/h).
History: First flight (prototype) 21 June 1938, (production C-54) 14 February 1942; final delivery (civil) post-war.
Users: (WWII) UK (RAF), US (AAF, Navy).

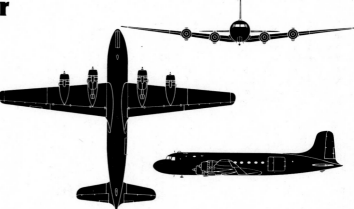

Above: Three-view of C-54 (all sub-types externally similar).

Development: The pre-war DC-4 did not prove a success, and eventually was sold to Japan (see Nakajima G5N), but in 1940 Douglas cut the DC-4 down in size and simplified it to produce a much better transport. In 1941 the production batch was taken over by the Army, and again altered for military use. Thus the first off the production line (there was no prototype of the new design) flew in olive drab. Ultimately 1,242 of these excellent machines were built, all having large freight doors and strong floors, about 44 removable seats, glider tow cleats and military gear throughout. The B had integral outer-wing tanks, the C was a VIP machine with electric hoist for President Roosevelt's wheelchair, and later marks (made mainly at Chicago) were convertible to several roles. Canadian Vickers bought a manufacturing licence, became Canadair in 1944 and finally built their DC-4s with Merlin engines. Post-war military versions took model sub-types up to C-54T, all rebuilds.

Right: Except for early production blocks, which were olive drab, all C-54s were delivered in shining metal finish, save only for the prominent black rubber de-icer boots on leading edges.

Douglas military DC-3 (C-47, Skytrain, Dakota)

C-47 and AC-47, R4D, C-53, Dakota, C-117, L2D and Li-2

Origin: Douglas Aircraft Company; built under licence by Showa and Nakajima, Japan, and (under direction of Lisunov bureau) Soviet Union.
Type: Utility transport (formerly also paratroop/glider tug): AC-47 air/ground weapon platform.
Engines: Usually two 1,200hp Pratt & Whitney R-1830-90D or -92 Twin Wasp 14-cylinder two-row radials; (C-117D) two 1,535hp Wright R-1820-80 Cyclone nine-cylinder radials; (Li-2) two 1,000hp M-62IR (Cyclone-derived) nine-cylinder radials; (L2D) two 1,050 or 1,300hp Mitsubishi Ki-43 or Ki-51 Kinsei 14-cylinder radials.
Dimensions: Span 95ft (28·96m); length 64ft 5½in (19·64m); height 16ft 11in (5·16m).
Weights: Empty, about 16,970lb (7700kg); loaded about 25,200lb (11,432kg); overload limit 33,000lb (14,969kg).
Performance: Maximum speed about 230mph (370km/h); initial climb, about 1,200ft (366m)/min; service ceiling 23,000ft (7000m); maximum range 2,125 miles (3420km).
Armament: (AC-47) usually three 7·62mm Miniguns; many other types of armament in other versions but none usually fitted.

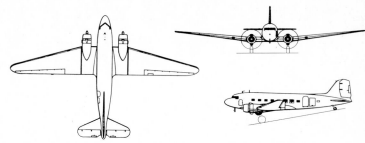

Above: Three-view of typical C-47 (all generally similar).

History: First flight (DST) 17 December 1935; first service delivery (C-41) October 1938.
Users: Australia, Bolivia, Brazil, China, France, Japan, New Zealand, South Africa, Soviet Union, UK (RAF, BOAC), US (AAC/AAF, Navy, Marines).

Development: When, in 1935, Douglas designer Arthur E. Raymond planned the Douglas Sleeper Transport (DST) as an enlarged and improved DC-2, he little thought that, as well as becoming the worldwide standard airliner of its day, it would be by far the most widely used military transport in history. During World War II there were numerous versions, some civil aircraft impressed into military use, some paratroopers and tugs and the vast majority utility C-47 versions with a strong cargo floor and large double doors. Oddities included a glider and a twin-float amphibian. US military production totalled 10,048 by June 1945, followed by small batches of redesigned Super DC-3 versions including the R4D-8 and C-117. Showa and Nakajima in Japan built about 571 of the L2D family and in the Soviet Union production of the Li-2 (with door on the right) is estimated to have exceeded 2,700. Many hundreds of these aircraft, most of them C-47s, remain in daily use in almost every air force (the RAF retired its last in 1970). Many serve as platforms for research projects and countermeasures and in Vietnam the AC-47 — called "Puff the Magic Dragon" — was developed in several versions to deliver suppressive fire against ground targets. Other important variants are the EC-47 series used for multi-spectral sensing and electronic reconnaissance.

Left: The C-47 in all versions was supremely reliable, and it had excellent wheelbrakes, but it needed two pilots to taxi safely in confined areas. Wheels-up landings were "a piece of cake".

Right: Old colour film plays tricks with shades, but there were two distinct olive shades for AAF transports, this C-47B Skytrain having the brown one. Engines were R-1830-90C.

Douglas SBD/A-24 Dauntless

SBD, A-24 Dauntless

Origin: Douglas Aircraft Company.
Type: Two-seat carrier-based (SBD) or land-based (A-24) dive bomber.
Engine: One 1,000hp Wright R-1820-32 or -52 or 1,200hp R-1820-60 or -66 Cyclone nine-cylinder radial.
Dimensions: Span 41ft 6in (12·65m); length 33ft (10·06m); height 12ft 11in (3·94m).
Weights: Empty, typically 6,535lb (2970kg); loaded 9,519—10,700lb (4320—4853kg).
Performance: (SBD-5): maximum speed 252mph (406km/h); initial climb 1,500ft (457m)/min; service ceiling 24,300ft (7400m); range (dive bomber) 456 miles (730km), (scout bomber) 773 miles (1240km).
Armament: One (later invariably two) 0·5in Browning machine guns fixed in nose, one (later two) 0·30in Brownings manually aimed from rear cockpit; one bomb or other store of up to 1,000lb (454kg) on swinging crutch under belly, outer-wing racks for two 100lb (45kg) bombs or, sometimes, two 250lb (113kg) bombs or depth charges.
History: First flight (XBT-1) July 1935; service delivery (XBT-1) 12 December 1935; (BT-1) 15 November 1937 to 19 October 1938; (XBT-2, Dauntless prototype) 23 July 1938; (SBD-1) 4 June 1940; termination of production 22 July 1944.
Users: Australia, Chile, France, Mexico, New Zealand, UK (RN, not operational), US (AAF, Navy, Marines).

Below: It is truly remarkable that the SBD, so similar to Britain's disastrous Battle, should have turned the whole tide of war in the Pacific. Note perforated dive brakes.

Development: In 1932 John K. Northrop set up his own company to specialise in the new technique of all-metal stressed-skin construction, though he retained close links with his former employer, Douglas Aircraft. His brilliant designer, Ed Heinemann, started in 1934 to develop a carrier-based dive-bomber for the new Navy carriers, basing the design on the established Northrop A-17A. The resulting Northrop BT-1 was ordered in quantity (54) in February 1936. It featured perforated split flaps and main gears folding backwards into large fairings. The last BT-1 was delivered in a greatly modified form, as the BT-2, with inward-retracting mainwheels, a 1,000hp Cyclone engine and many refinements. By this time Northrop had become the El Segundo division of Douglas and in consequence the production BT-2 was redesignated SBD-1. From June 1940 until four years later this was one of the most important US combat aircraft, indeed, in the first half of 1942 it saw more action than any other American type. After the 57 SBD-1s came 87 SBD-2s with greater fuel capacity, 584 SBD-3s with armour and self-sealing tanks (and 168 more for the Army with pneumatic tailwheel and no hook), 780 SBD-4 (24V electrics) plus 170 for the Army, 3,024 SBD-5s with 1,200hp engine (including 615 as Army A-24Bs) and 451 SBD-6 (1,350hp), to make the total 5,936. Dauntless sank more Japanese shipping than any other Allied weapon, stopped the Imperial Fleet at Midway and played a major role at the Coral Sea and Solomons actions.

Above: This squadron probably has the SBD-5 or -6, but differences between sub-types were mainly internal. ASV radar was introduced with the -4, together with radio navaids.

Below: Side elevation of an SBD-5, with 1,000lb GP bomb, assigned to shore-based VMSB-231, Marine Air Group 22.

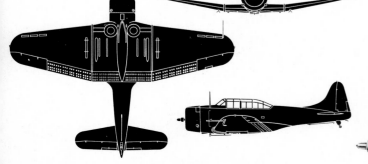

Above: Three-view typical of all SBD/A-24 variants.

Douglas TBD Devastator

TBD-1 Devastator

Origin: Douglas Aircraft Company.
Type: Three-seat carrier-based torpedo bomber.
Engine: One 850hp Pratt & Whitney R-1830-64 Twin Wasp 14-cylinder two-row radial.
Dimensions: Span 50ft (15·24m); length 35ft 6in (10·82m); height 15ft 1in (4·6m).
Weights: Empty 7,195lb (3264kg); maximum loaded 10,194lb (4622kg).
Performance: Maximum speed 206mph (332km/h); initial climb at maximum weight 900ft (274m)/min; service ceiling 19,700ft (6000m); range with full weapon load 435 miles (700km).
Armament: One 0·30in Colt-Browning fixed on right side of nose, one 0·5in manually aimed in rear cockpit, single 21in (1,000lb 454kg) Bliss-Leavitt torpedo recessed into belly, light bomb racks under wings for total additional load of 500lb (227kg).
History: First flight (XTBD-1) January 1935; production delivery 25 June 1937.
User: US (Navy).

Development: In the early 1930s the US Navy ordered new aircraft carriers, the *Ranger, Yorktown* and *Enterprise*. Among their complement were to be squadrons of torpedo bombers and on 30 June 1934 orders were placed for two prototypes of rival designs. One was the Great Lakes XTBG-1, rather similar to the later British Swordfish. The other was the first cantilever monoplane designed for such a duty, the Douglas XTBD-1. The monoplane started with the drawback of being radically new, though the wing was very thick, the retracted main wheels protruded far enough for safe landings and the landing speed was only 59mph. The large canopy over the pilot, radio operator and gunner opened into six sections for "open cockpit" vision, and the all-round performance of the monoplane was superior. Despite competition from another monoplane contender, on 3 February 1936, the Douglas won the production order for 110 aircraft, then the largest peacetime order for aircraft placed by the US Navy. The production TBD had a taller canopy with crash pylon, power-folding wings and other changes. Altogether 129 were delivered, and over 100 were still the only carrier-based torpedo bombers in US service at the time of Pearl Harbor. Named Devastator, they immediately went into violent action, bombing and torpedoing almost on a round-the-clock basis. The middle crewmember aimed the torpedo, sighting through doors in the belly and from a prone position. In the Marshalls and Gilberts these aircraft proved formidable, but they were obsolescent and in the Battle of Midway 35 were shot down by flak and Zeros in a single action. The Devastator was soon afterwards replaced by the Avenger.

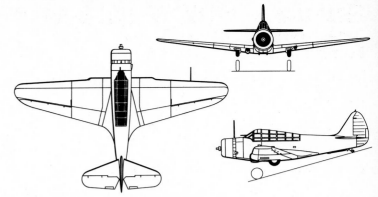

Above: Three-view of TBD-1 Devastator.

Above: In its day the TBD was an excellent aircraft, but that day was drawing swiftly to a close when the US Navy found itself at war on 7 December 1941. Its wing area was by then appropriate to aircraft of twice the weight and three times the power of the very early-series Twin Wasp engine.

Fairchild M-62 Cornell family

PT-19, -23 and -26, Cornell II

Origin: Fairchild Aircraft Division, Hagerstown, Maryland; built under licence by Aeronca, Howard, St Louis and Fleet (Canada).
Type: Primary trainer.
Engine: (19) 175hp Ranger 6-440C-2 inverted six-in-line aircooled, (23) 220hp Continental R-670-11 seven-cylinder radial, (26,Cornell II) 200hp Ranger L-440-7.
Dimensions: Span (19,23) 36ft 11¼in (11·26m), (26) 36ft 0in (10·97m); length (19,26) 27ft 11½in (8·52m), (23) 25ft 10¾in (7·90m); height 7ft 6in (2·29m).
Weights: Empty (23) 2,046lb (928kg), (26) 2,022lb (917kg); maximum (23) 2,747lb (1246kg), (26) 2,741lb (1243kg).
Performance: Maximum speed (typical) 126mph (203km/h); typical cruise 110mph (177km/h); typical range 430 miles (692km).
History: First flight (19) 1939; final delivery (23, 26) May 1944.
Users: (WWII) Argentina, Brazil, Canada, Chile, Colombia, Ecuador, Mexico, Norway, Paraguay, S Africa, S Rhodesia, UK (RAF), Uruguay, US (AAC/AAF).

Development: Fairchild's M-62 was a simple but quite large trainer with wooden wing (with manual flaps) and steel-tube/fabric fuselage. It immediately attracted export orders, usually with the Warner Super Scarab engine, but the US Army Air Corps adopted it in 1939 with the Ranger. The PT-19 was built by Fairchild and Aeronca, the radial-engined 23 in vast numbers by Howard, Aeronca and St Louis, and the 26 with enclosed cockpits by Fleet, for the Commonwealth Air Training Plan. Hundreds were used in S Rhodesia, where in 1946 the author supervised the destruction of 97 straight out of their crates. Total production was 7,250 in the USA and about 1,150 in Canada.

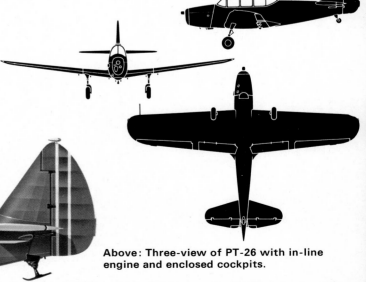

Above: Three-view of PT-26 with in-line engine and enclosed cockpits.

Left: Though little-used by US forces, the PT-26 variant was the most important to other Allies and served in vast numbers in the RAF and RCAF as the Cornell II. One batch equipped the "Little Norway" training school in Canada, with RNorAF insignia, cockpit heaters and often skis (here tail-ski only).

Grumman F4F/FM Wildcat

G-36, Martlet, F4F-1 to -4 and Eastern Aircraft FM-1 and -2

Origin: Grumman Aircraft Engineering Corporation; also built by Eastern Aircraft.

Type: Single-seat naval fighter.

Engine: (XF4F-2) one 1,050hp Pratt & Whitney R-1830-66 Twin Wasp 14-cylinder two-row radial; (G-36A, Martlet I (Wildcat I)) one 1,200hp Wright R-1820-G205A Cyclone nine-cylinder radial; (F4F-3) 1,200hp R-1830-76; (F4F-4 and FM-1 (Wildcat V)) R-1830-86; (FM-2 (Wildcat VI)) 1,350hp R-1820-56.

Dimensions: Span 38ft 0in (11·6m); length 28ft 9in to 28ft 11in (FM-2, 28ft 10in, 8·5m); height 11ft 11in (3·6m).

Weights: Empty (F4F-3) 4,425lb; (F4F-4) 4,649lb; (FM-2) 4,900lb (2226kg); loaded (F4F-3) 5,876lb; (F4F-4) 6,100lb rising to 7,952lb (3607kg) with final FM-1s; (FM-2) 7,412lb.

Performance: Maximum speed (F4F-3) 325mph (523km/h); (F4F-4, FM-1) 318mph (509km/h); (FM-2) 332mph (534km/h); initial climb, typically 2,000ft (610m)/min (3,300ft/min in early versions, 1,920 in main production and over 2,000 for FM-2); service ceiling, typically 35,000ft (10,670m) (more in light early versions); range, typically 900 miles (1448km).

Armament: (XF4F-2) two 0·5in Colt-Brownings in fuselage; (F4F-3) four 0·5in in outer wings; (F4F-4 and subsequent) six 0·5in in outer wings; (F4F-4, FM-1 and FM-2) underwing racks for two 250lb (113kg) bombs.

History: First flight (XF4F-2) 2 September 1937; (XF4F-3) 12 February 1939; production (G-36 and F4F-3) February 1940; (FM-2) March 1943; final delivery August 1945.

Users: France (FFL), Greece, UK (RN), US (Navy, Marines).

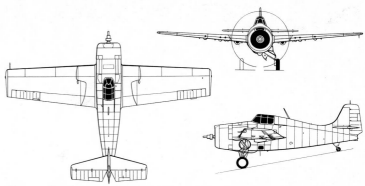

Above: Three-view of F4F-4 (most other versions similar).

Development: Designed as a biplane to continue Grumman's very successful F3F series of single-seat carrier fighters, the XF4F-1 was re-planned on the drawing board in the summer of 1936 as a mid-wing monoplane. Though this machine, the XF4F-2, lost out to the Brewster F2A Buffalo, Grumman continued with the XF4F-3 with a more powerful engine and in early 1939 received a French Aéronavale order for 100, the US Navy following with 54 in August. The French aircraft were diverted to Britain and named Martlet I. Production built up with both Twin Wasp and Cyclone engines, folding wings being introduced with the F4F-4, of which Grumman delivered 1,169 plus 220 Martlet IVs for the Fleet Air Arm. Eastern Aircraft Division of General Motors very quickly tooled up and delivered 839 FM-1s and 311 Martlet Vs, the British name then being changed to the US name of Wildcat. Grumman switched to the Avenger, Hellcat and other types, but made F4F-7 reconnaissance versions, weighing 10,328lb and having a 24-hour endurance, as well as a floatplane version. Eastern took over the final mark, the powerful and effective FM-2, delivering 4,777 of this type (including 340 Wildcat VI) in 13 months. A Martlet I shot down a Ju 88 on Christmas Day 1940, and an F4F-3 of VMF-211 destroyed a Japanese bomber at Wake Island on 9 December 1941. Each event was the first of thousands of furious actions from which this quite old fighter emerged with a splendid reputation. Wildcats were especially valuable for their ability to operate from small escort carriers, the pioneer work having been done with British Martlets based in November 1940 on the 5,000 ton captured German vessel *Audacity* on which a flat deck had been built. Noted for their strength and manoeuvrability. Wildcats even sank Japanese submarines and a cruiser.

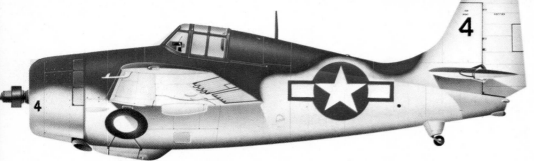

Above: Part of a squadron of Eastern Aircraft FM-1 Wildcats over the Pacific. All FM models carried only four 0·5in guns.

Left: A US Navy F4F-4 (Twin Wasp and six guns) in 1944-45 colouring.

Below: A Royal Navy Wildcat V (with four guns, and in this case with the Cyclone cowled as in the later FM-2) pictured aboard a Fleet carrier of the Royal Navy.

Grumman F6F Hellcat

F6F-1 to -5 Hellcat

Origin: Grumman Aircraft Engineering Corporation.
Type: Single-seat naval fighter; later versions, fighter-bombers and night fighters.
Engine: Early production, one 2,000hp Pratt & Whitney R-2800-10 Double Wasp 18-cylinder two-row radial; from January 1944 (final F6F-3 batch) two-thirds equipped with 2,200hp (water-injection rating) R-2800-10W.
Dimensions: Span 42ft 10in (13·05m); length 33ft 7in (10·2m); height 13ft 1in (3·99m).
Weights: Empty (F6F-3) 9,042lb (4101kg); loaded (F6F-3) 12,186lb (5528kg) clean, 13,228lb (6000kg) maximum, (F6F-5N) 14,250lb (6443kg).
Performance: Maximum speed (F6F-3, -5, clean) 376mph (605km/h); (-5N) 366mph (590km/h); initial climb (typical) 3,240ft (990m)/min;

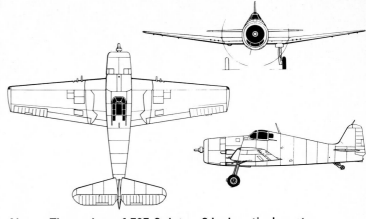

Above: Three-view of F6F-3; later -3 had vertical mast.

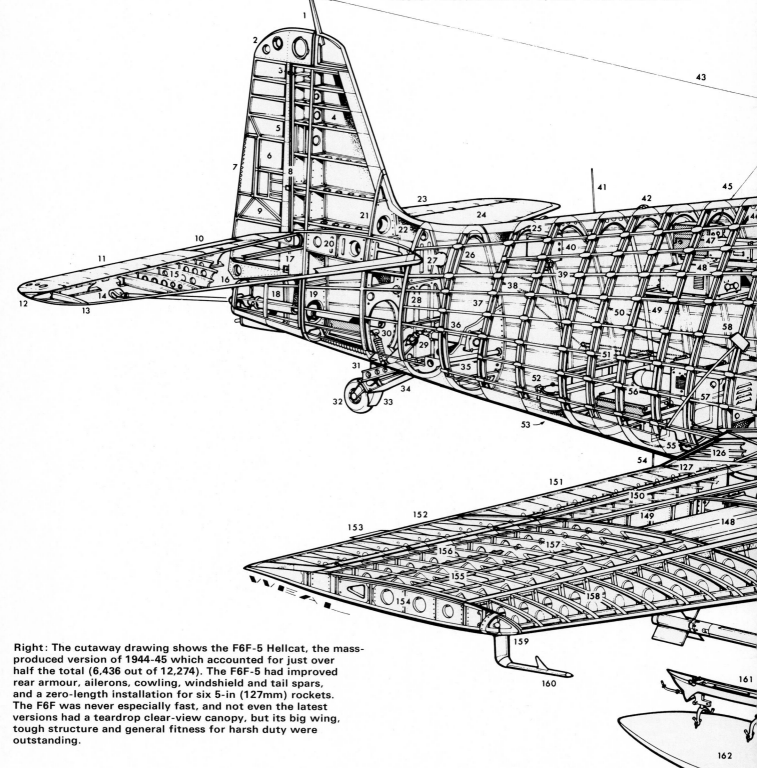

Right: The cutaway drawing shows the F6F-5 Hellcat, the mass-produced version of 1944-45 which accounted for just over half the total (6,436 out of 12,274). The F6F-5 had improved rear armour, ailerons, cowling, windshield and tail spars, and a zero-length installation for six 5-in (127mm) rockets. The F6F was never especially fast, and not even the latest versions had a teardrop clear-view canopy, but its big wing, tough structure and general fitness for harsh duty were outstanding.

**Grumman F6F Hellcat
cutaway drawing key:**

1 Radio mast
2 Rudder balance
3 Rudder upper hinge
4 Aluminium alloy fin ribs
5 Rudder post
6 Rudder structure
7 Rudder trim tab
8 Rudder middle hinge
9 Diagonal stiffeners
10 Aluminium alloy elevator trim tab
11 Fabric-covered (and taped) elevator surfaces
12 Elevator balance
13 Flush riveted leading-edge strip
14 Arrester hook (extended)
15 Tailplane ribs
16 Tail navigation (running) light
17 Rudder lower hinge
18 Arrester hook (stowed)
19 Fin main-spar lower cut-out
20 Tailplane end rib
21 Fin forward spar
22 Fuselage/fin root fairing
23 Port elevator
24 Aluminium alloy-skinned tailplane
25 Section light
26 Fuselage aft frame
27 Control access
28 Bulkhead
29 Tailwheel hydraulic shock-absorber
30 Tailwheel centering mechanism
31 Tailwheel steel mounting arm
32 Rearward-retracting tailwheel (hard rubber tyre)
33 Fairing
34 Steel plate door fairing
35 Tricing sling support tube (for hoisting aboard carrier)
36 Hydraulic actuating cylinder
37 Flanged ring fuselage frames
38 Control cable runs
39 Fuselage longerons
40 Relay box
41 Dorsal rod antenna
42 Dorsal recognition light
43 Radio aerial
44 Radio mast
45 Aerial lead-in
46 Dorsal frame stiffeners
47 Junction box
48 Radio equipment (upper rack)
49 Radio shelf
50 Control cable runs
51 Transverse brace
52 Remote radio compass
53 Ventral recognition lights (3)
54 Ventral rod antenna
55 Destructor device
56 Accumulator
57 Radio equipment (lower rack)
58 Entry hand/footholds
59 Engine water injection tank
60 Canopy track
61 Water filler neck
62 Rear-view window
63 Rearward-sliding cockpit canopy (open)
64 Headrest
65 Pilot's head/shoulder armour
66 Canopy sill (reinforced)
67 Fire-extinguisher
68 Oxygen bottle (port fuselage wall)
69 Water tank mounting
70 Underfloor self-sealing fuel tank (60 US gal/227 litres)
71 Armoured bulkhead
72 Starboard console
73 Pilot's seat
74 Hydraulic handpump
75 Fuel filler cap and neck
76 Rudder pedals
77 Central console
78 Control column
79 Chart board (horizontal stowage)
80 Instrument panel
81 Panel coaming
82 Reflector gunsight
83 Rear-view mirror
84 Armoured glass windshield
85 Deflection plate (pilot forward protection)
86 Main bulkhead armour-plated upper section with hoisting sling attachments port and starboard
87 Aluminium alloy aileron trim tab
88 Fabric covered (and taped) aileron surfaces
89 Flush riveted outer wing skin
90 Aluminium alloy sheet wing tip (riveted to wing outer rib)
91 Port navigation (running) light
92 Formed leading-edge (approach/landing light and camera gun inboard)
93 Fixed cowling panel
94 Armour plate (oil tank forward protection)
95 Oil tank (19 US gal/72 litres)
96 Welded engine mount fittings
97 Fuselage forward bulkhead
98 Aileron control linkage
99 Engine accessories bay
100 Engine mounting frame (hydraulic fluid reservoir attached to port frames)
101 Controllable cooling gills
102 Cowling ring (removable servicing/access panels)
103 Pratt & Whitney R-2800-10W twin-row radial air-cooled engine
104 Nose ring profile
105 Reduction gear housing
106 Three-blade Hamilton Standard Hydromatic controllable pitch propeller
107 Propeller hub
108 Engine oil cooler (centre) and supercharger intercooler (outer sections) intakes
109 Oil cooler deflection plate under-protection
110 Oil cooler duct
111 Intercooler intake duct
112 Mainwheel fairing
113 Port mainwheel
114 Cooler outlet and fairing
115 Auxiliary tank support/attachment arms
116 Exhaust cluster
117 Supercharger housing
118 Exhaust outlet scoop
119 Wing front spar web
120 Wing front spar/fuselage attachment bolts
121 Undercarriage mounting/pivot point on front spar
122 Inter-spar self-sealing fuel tanks (port and starboard: 87·5 US gal/331 litres each)
123 Wing rear spar/fuselage attachment bolts
124 Structural end rib
125 Slotted wing flap profile
126 Wing flap centre-section
127 Wing fold line
128 Starboard wheel well (double-plate reinforced edges)
129 Gun bay
130 Removable diagonal brace strut
131 Three 0·5-in (12,7-mm) Colt Browning machine guns
132 Auxiliary tank aft support
133 Blast tubes
134 Folding wing joint (upper surface)
135 Machine-gun barrels
136 Fairing
137 Undercarriage actuating strut
138 Mainwheel leg oleo hydraulic shock strut
139 Auxiliary tank sling/brace
140 Long-range auxiliary fuel tank (jettisonable)
141 Mainwheel aluminium alloy fairing
142 Forged steel torque link
143 Cast magnesium wheel
144 Low pressure balloon tyre
145 Underwing 5-in (127mm) air-to-ground RPs
146 Mark V zero-length rocket launcher installation
147 Canted wing front spar
148 Inter-spar ammunition box bar (lower surface access)
149 Wing rear spar (normal to plane of wing)
150 Rear sub spar
151 Wing fold outer-section
152 Frise-type aileron
153 Aileron balance tab
154 Wing outer rib
155 Wing lateral stiffeners
156 Aileron spar
157 Wing outer-section ribs
158 Leading-edge rib cut-outs
159 Starboard navigation (running) light
160 Pitot head
161 Underwing stores pylon (mounted on fixed centre-section inboard of mainwheel leg)
162 Auxiliary fuel tank

► service ceiling (÷3) 37,500ft (11,430m); (-5N) 36,700ft (11,185m); range on internal fuel (typical) 1,090 miles (1755km).

Armament: Standard, six 0·5in Brownings in outer wings with 400 rounds each; a few -5N and -5 Hellcats had two 20mm and four 0·5in. Underwing attachments for six rockets, and centre-section pylons for 2,000lb of bombs.

History: First flight (R-2600) 26 June 1942; (same aircraft, R-2800) 30 July 1942; (production F6F-3) 4 October 1942; production delivery (F6F-3) 16 January 1943; final delivery November 1945.

Users: UK (RN), US (Navy, Marines).

Development: Though pugnacious rather than elegant, the Hellcat was a truly war-winning aircraft. It was designed and developed with great speed, mass-produced at a rate seldom equalled by any other single aircraft factory and used to such good effect that, from the very day of its appearance, the Allies were winning the air war in the Pacific. It began as the XF6F-1, a natural development of the F4F Wildcat with R-2600 Double Cyclone engine. Within a month the more powerful Double Wasp had been substituted and in the autumn of 1942 the production line took shape inside a completely new plant that was less advanced in construction than the Hellcats inside it! This line flowed at an extraordinary rate, helped by the essential rightness of the Hellcat and lack of major engineering changes during subsequent sub-types. Deliveries in the years 1942–45 inclusive were 10, 2,545, 6,139 and 3,578, a total of 12,272 (excluding two prototypes) of which 11,000 were delivered in exactly two years. These swarms of big, beefy fighters absolutely mastered the Japanese, destroying more than 6,000 hostile aircraft (4,947 by USN carrier squadrons, 209 by land-based USMC units and the rest by Allied Hellcat squadrons). The Fleet Air Arm, which originally chose the name Gannet, used Hellcats in Europe as well as throughout the Far East. Unusual features of the F6F were its 334 sq ft of square-tipped wing, with a distinct kink, and backward-retracting landing gear. The F6F-3N and -5N were night fighters with APS-6 radar on a wing pod; the -5K was a drone and the -5P a photographic reconnaissance version. After VJ-day hundreds were sold to many nations.

Above: F6F goes round again after getting a wave-off by the batsman — for obvious reasons, because the deck of this escort carrier is obstructed by another Hellcat.

Below: F6F-3 Hellcat pilots waiting to start their engines for a mission, aboard a US Navy carrier in the Pacific. The F6F-5 differed in having extra armour, better cowling and other details.

Above: A Hellcat takes off from USS Enterprise near the end of the war.

Right: Formation of US Navy Hellcats, probably from Fighter Squadron VF-8.

Below: A Naval photographer catches an F6F as it comes in to USS Yorktown.

Grumman F7F Tigercat

F7F-1 to -4N Tigercat

Origin: Grumman Aircraft Engineering Corporation.
Type: Single-seat or two-seat fighter bomber or night fighter (-4N for carrier operation).
Engines: Two Pratt & Whitney R-2800-22W or -34W Double Wasp 18-cylinder two-row radials each rated at 2,100hp (dry) or 2,400hp (water injection).
Dimensions: Span 51ft 6in (15·7m); length (most) 45ft 4in or 45ft 4½in (13·8m); (-3N, -4N) 46ft 10in (14·32m); height (-1, -2) 15ft 2in (4·6m); (-3, -4) 16ft 7in (5·06m).
Weights: Empty (-1) 13,100lb (5943kg); (-3N, -4N) 16,270lb (7379kg); loaded (-1) 22,560lb (10,235kg); (-2N) 26,194lb (11,880kg); (-3) 25,720lb; (-4N) 26,167lb.
Performance: Maximum speed (-1) 427mph (689km/h); (-2N) 421mph; (-3) 435mph; (-4N) 430mph; initial climb (-1) 4,530ft (1380m)/min; service ceiling (-1) 36,200ft; (-2N) 39,800ft (12,131m); (-3) 40,700ft; (-4N) 40,450ft; range on internal fuel (-1) 1,170 miles (1885km); (-2N) 960 miles; (-3) 1,200 miles; (-4N) 810 miles.
Armament: Basic (-1) four 0·5in Browning each with 300 rounds in the nose and four 20mm M-2 cannon each with 200 rounds in the wing roots;

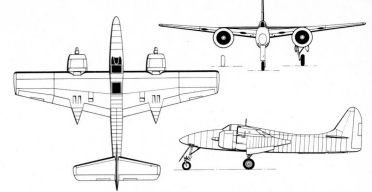

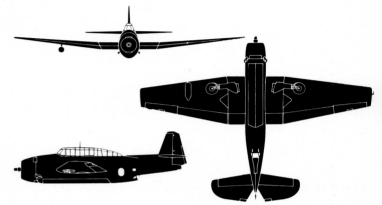

Above: Three-view of F7F-3 (most -3 had long NF or photo nose).

outer-wing pylons for six rockets or two 1,000 lb (454kg) bombs; alternatively, one 21in torpedo on fuselage centreline. (-3), nose guns only; (-2N, -3N, -4N) wing guns only.
History: First flight (XF7F-1) December 1943; first service delivery October 1944; final delivery, December 1946.

Grumman TBF/TBM Avenger

TBF and Eastern Aircraft TBM series

Origin: Grumman Aircraft Engineering Corporation; also built by Eastern Aircraft.
Type: Originally, three-seat torpedo bomber; later ASW (anti-submarine warfare) aircraft and AEW (airborne early warning) aircraft.
Engine: One 1,700hp Wright R-2600-8 or -20 Double Cyclone 14-cylinder two-row radial.
Dimensions: Span 54ft 2in (16·5m); length (to TBM-3) 40ft 0in (12·2m); (TBM-3E) 40ft 11½in (12·48m); height 16ft 5in (5m).
Weights: Empty (TBF-1) 10,100lb (4580kg); (TBM-3) 10,545lb (4787kg); loaded (TBF-1) 15,905lb (7214kg); (TBM-3) 18,250lb (8278kg); (TBM-3E) 17,895lb (8117kg).
Performance: Maximum speed (TBF-1) 278mph (445km/h); (TBM-3) 267mph (430km/h); initial climb (TBF-1) 1,075ft (376m)/min; service ceiling (TBF, TBM-1 to -3) about 23,400ft (7132m); (TBM-3E) 30,100ft; range with full weapon load, 1,010–1,215 miles (1600–1950km); ferry range, 2,530 miles (4072km).
Armament: (TBF-1, TBM-1) one 0·30in Browning in upper forward fuselage, one 0·5in in dorsal power turret and one 0·30in manually aimed in rear ventral position; internal bay for one 22in torpedo or 2,000lb (907kg) of bombs; (TBF-1C, TBM-1C, TBM-3) as above plus one 0·5in in each outer wing and underwing racks for eight 60lb (27kg) rockets. Most subsequent versions unarmed, or fitted for ASW weapons only.
History: First flight (XTBF-1) 1 August 1941; service delivery 30 January

Below: A crowded flight deck somewhere in the Pacific in late 1942. Most of the picture is occupied by TBFs, but in the extreme foreground are F6F Hellcat fighters, while at the rear (wings spread) are a squadron of SBD Dauntless scout-bombers.

Above: Three-view of Eastern Aircraft TBM-3 (no turret).

1942; final delivery from new production, September 1945; final delivery of rebuild, August 1954.
Users: (wartime) New Zealand, UK (RN), US (Navy, Marines).

Development: Grumman's outstanding design and engineering staff, under W. T. (Bill) Schwendler, designed and developed this big and extremely useful torpedo bomber very quickly and it became one of the key aircraft in the Pacific war. Two prototypes were ordered on 8 April 1940 and large numbers were in action at the Battle of Midway just over two years later. From the start the TBF was robust and well equipped and one could not help comparing it with the British Barracuda which lacked power, self-defence and a weapon bay. Fortunately a proportion of deliveries went to the Fleet Air Arm, which originally considered the name Tarpon before

Users: UK (RN), US (Navy, Marines).

Development: Ordered on the same day as the F6F Hellcat prototypes in June 1941 the F7F was one of the boldest designs in the history of combat aircraft. During the preceding two years the US Navy had keenly studied air war in Europe and noted that the things that appeared to count were the obvious ones; engine power, armament and protective armour and self-sealing tanks. At a time when the average US Navy fighter had 1,000hp and two machine guns the Bureau of Aeronautics asked Grumman to build a fighter with more than 4,000hp and a weight of fire more than 200 times as great. The company had embarked on a venture along these lines in 1938 with the XF5F, which remained a one-off prototype that was judged not worth the cost and incompatible with Navy carriers. In contrast the F7F was planned on a basis of knowledge and though dramatically heavier and faster than any previous carrier aircraft it was matched with the deck of the large Midway class carriers then under construction. Most, however, were ordered for the Marine Corps for use from land. The F7F-1 of which 34 were built, were single seaters with APS-6 radar in a wing pod. The 66 F7F-2Ns followed, with nose radar in place of guns and the observer in place of the rear fuel tank. The -3 introduced the -34W engine and so had a larger tail; most of the 250 built were -3N night fighters or -3P photographic aircraft. The final models were strengthened -4s, cleared for carrier use, the whole batch being -4Ns. Tigercats arrived at a time when emphasis was rapidly switching to the jet.

Above: A rare bird, the single-seat F7F-3, which was virtually similar to the original F7F-1 but with more power and increased fuel capacity. Most -3s had a nose full of cameras or radar.

adopting the US Navy name. Of 2,293 Grumman-built aircraft delivered by December 1943, 402 went to the RN and 63 to the RNZAF. Eastern Aircraft, the second source, delivered 2,882 of the TBM-1 and -1C type, before switching to the slightly modified -3 in April 1944. Many -3s had no turret, all had strengthened wings for rockets or a radar pod, and no fewer than 4,664 were delivered by Eastern in 14 months. After 1945 development suddenly blossomed out into new versions, produced as conversions. The TBM-3E was packed with ASW search and attack equipment, the TBM-3W and -3W2 were grotesque "guppy" type early-warners with huge belly radar, the -3U was a tug and the -3R a COD (carrier on-board delivery) transport with seven passenger seats. The Fleet Air Arm put 100 TBM-3E anti-submarine versions into use as the Avenger AS.4 in 1953 and about 500 more post-war variants served with the USN, RCN, Aéronavale, Japan and Netherlands.

Right: Catapult takeoff with flap from a US Navy carrier.

Below: Air and ground crews of the Fleet Air Arm hustle before a bombing raid by Avenger IIs from a Pacific base in 1945.

Lockheed Model 414 (A-29, PBO) Hudson

Hudson I to VI, A-28, A-29, AT-18, C-63 and PBO-1

Origin: Lockheed Aircraft Corporation.
Type: Reconnaissance bomber and utility.
Engines: (Hudson I, II) two 1,100hp Wright GR-1820-G102A nine-cylinder radials; (Hudson III, A-29, PBO-1) two 1,200hp GR-1820-G205A, (Hudson IV, V, VI and A-28) two 1,200hp Pratt & Whitney R-1830-S3C3-G, S3C4-G or -67 14-cylinder two-row radials.
Dimensions: Span 65ft 6in (19·96m); length 44ft 4in (13·51m); height 11ft 10½in (3·62m).
Weights: Empty (I) 12,000lb (5443kg); (VI) 12,929lb (5864kg); maximum loaded (I) 18,500lb (8393kg); (VI) 22,360lb (10,142kg).
Performance: Maximum speed (I) 246mph (397km/h); (VI) 261mph (420km/h); initial climb 1,200ft (366m)/min; service ceiling 24,500ft (7468m); range (I) 1,960 miles (3150km); (VI) 2,160 miles (3475km).
Armament: (Typical RAF Hudson in GR role) seven 0·303in Brownings in nose (two, fixed), dorsal turret (two), beam windows and ventral hatch; internal bomb/depth charge load up to 750lb (341kg).
History: First flight (civil Model 14) 29 July 1937; (Hudson I) 10 December 1938; squadron delivery February 1939; USAAC and USN delivery, October 1941.
Users: Australia, Brazil, Canada, China, Netherlands, New Zealand, UK (RAF, BOAC), US (AAC/AAF, Navy).

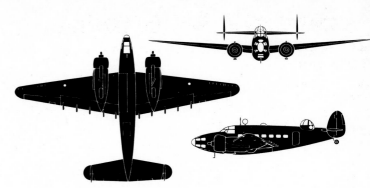

Above: Three-view of Hudson I (all Cyclone-powered similar).

Development: In 1938 the British Purchasing Commission was established in Washington to seek out US aircraft that could serve with the RAF and Royal Navy and help bolster British strength beyond the then-small capacity of the British aircraft industry. One of the urgent needs was for a modern long-range reconnaissance and navigation trainer aircraft and Lockheed Aircraft, at Burbank — just climbing out of the Depression — hastily built a mock-up of their Model 14 airliner to meet the requirement. An order for 200 aircraft, many times bigger than any previous order ever received by Lockheed, was fulfilled swiftly and efficiently. The order was many times multiplied and the versatile Hudson served with several RAF commands in many theatres of war. On 8 October 1939 a Hudson over Jutland shot down the first German aircraft claimed by the RAF in World War II. In February 1940 another discovered the prison ship *Altmark* in a Norwegian fjord and directed naval forces to the rescue. Over Dunkirk Hudsons acted as dog-fighters, in August 1941 one accepted the surrender of U-boat *U-570*, and from 1942 many made secret landings in France to deliver or collect agents or supplies. Hudsons of later marks carried ASV radar, rocket launchers and lifeboats. Total deliveries were 2,584 including about 490 armed versions for the US Army, 20 PBOs for the Navy and 300 AT-18 crew trainers. From this fine basic design stemmed the more powerful Vega Ventura bomber and ocean patrol aircraft and the PV-2 Harpoon at almost twice the weight of the Hudson I.

Below: Hudson GR.V (Twin Wasp engines) serving with 48 Sqn of RAF Coastal Command.

Above: This Cyclone-powered Hudson of the RAF is painted in post-1941 insignia but not in the expected dark sea grey and white of Coastal Command. Many served as transports.

Below: The Hudson was a useful utility transport, with plenty of room, high performance and long range. This Mk VI is being refuelled at an airfield in West Africa.

Lockheed P-38 Lightning

XP-38 to P-38M, F-4 and F-5, RP and TP conversions

Origin: Lockheed Aircraft Corporation.
Type: Single-seat long-range fighter (see text for variations).
Engines: Two Allison V-1710 vee-12 liquid-cooled; (YP-38) 1,150hp V-1710-27/29 (all P-38 engines handed with opposite propeller rotation, hence pairs of engine sub-type numbers); (P-38E to G) 1,325hp V-1710-49/52 or 51/55; (P-38H and J) 1,425hp V-1710-89/91; (P-38L and M) 1,600hp V-1710-111/113.
Dimensions: Span 52ft (15·86m); length 37ft 10in (11·53m); (F-5G, P-38M and certain "droop-snoot" conversions fractionally longer); height 12ft 10in (3·9m).
Weights: Empty, varied from 11,000lb (4990kg) in YP to average of 12,700lb (5766kg), with heaviest sub-types close to 14,000lb (6350kg); maximum loaded, (YP) 14,348lb (6508kg); (D) 15,500lb; (E) 15,482lb; (F) 18,000lb; (G) 19,800lb; (H) 20,300lb; (L, M) 21,600lb (9798kg).
Performance: Maximum speed (all) 391–414mph (630–666km/h); initial climb (all) about 2,850ft (870m)/min; service ceiling (up to G) 38,000–40,000ft; (H, J, L) 44,000ft (13,410m); range on internal fuel 350–460 miles (563–740km); range at 30,000ft with maximum fuel (late models) 2,260 miles (3650km).
Armament: See text.
History: First flight (XP-38) 27 January 1939; (YP-38) 16 September 1940; service delivery (USAAC P-38) 8 June 1941; (F-4) March 1942; (P-38F) September 1942; final delivery September 1945.
Users: France, UK (RAF, briefly), US (AAC/AAF).

Development: In February 1937 the US Army Air Corps issued a specification for a long-range interceptor (pursuit) and escort fighter, calling for a speed of 360mph at 20,000ft and endurance at this speed of one hour. Lockheed, which had never built a purely military design, jumped in with both feet and created a revolutionary fighter bristling with innovations and posing considerable technical risks. Powered by two untried Allison engines, with GEC turbochargers recessed into the tops of the tail booms, it had a tricycle landing gear, small central nacelle mounting a 23mm Madsen cannon and four 0·5in Brownings firing parallel directly ahead of the pilot, twin fins, Fowler flaps, cooling radiators on the flanks of the booms and induction intercoolers in the wing leading edges. This box of tricks ran into a ditch on its first taxi test, and two weeks after first flight undershot at Mitchell Field, NY, and was demolished. What made headlines, however, was that it had flown to New York in 7hr 2min, with two refuelling stops, demonstrating a performance which in 1939 seemed beyond belief. The enthusiasm of the Air Corps overcame the doubts and high cost and by 1941 the first YP-38 was being tested, with a 37mm Oldsmobile cannon, two 0·5s and two Colt 0·3s. Thirteen YPs were followed on the Burbank line by 20 P-38s, with one 37mm and four 0·5, plus armour and, in the 36 D models, self-sealing tanks. In March 1940 the British Purchasing Commission had ordered 143 of this type, with the 37mm replaced by a 20mm Hispano and far greater ammunition capacity. The State Department prohibited export of the F2 Allison engine and RAF aircraft, called Lightning I,

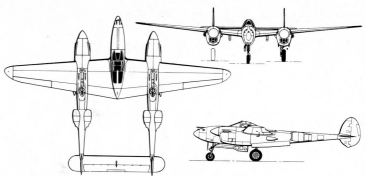

Above: Three-view of the mass-produced P-38J.

had early C15 engines without turbochargers, both having right-hand rotation (P-38s had propellers turning outward). The result was poor and the RAF rejected these machines, which were later brought up to US standard. The E model adopted the British name Lightning and the RAF Hispano gun. Within minutes of the US declaration of war, on 7 December 1941, an E shot down an Fw 200C near Iceland, and the P-38 was subsequently in the thick of fighting in North Africa, North West Europe and the Pacific. The F was the first to have inner-wing pylons for 1,000lb bombs, torpedoes, tanks or other stores. By late 1943 new G models were being flown to Europe across the North Atlantic, while in the Pacific 16 aircraft of the 339th Fighter Squadron destroyed Admiral Yamamoto's aircraft 550 miles from their base at Guadalcanal. The J had the intercoolers moved under the engines, changing the appearance, providing room for 55 extra gallons of fuel in the outer wings. Later J models had hydraulically boosted ailerons, but retained the wheel-type lateral control instead of a stick. The L, with higher war emergency power, could carry 4,000lb of bombs or ten rockets, and often formations would bomb under the direction of a lead-ship converted to droop-snoot configuration with a bombardier in the nose. Hundreds were built as F-4 or F-5 photographic aircraft, and the M was a two-seat night fighter with ASH radar pod under the nose. Lightnings towed gliders, operated on skis, acted as fast ambulances (carrying two stretcher cases) and were used for many special ECM missions. Total production was 9,942 and the P-38 made up for slightly inferior manoeuvrability by its range, reliability and multi-role effectiveness.

Above: The first sub-type to have inner-wing pylons was the P-38F.

Left: P-38F-5 from 347th FG, detached to the 13th Air Force at Guadalcanal.

Below: The deep engines of the much more numerous later models are seen in this unarmed photo F-5E.

Lockheed PV-1/B-34 Ventura

Vega 37, Ventura I to V, B-34 Lexington, B-37, PV-1 and -3 and PV-2 Harpoon

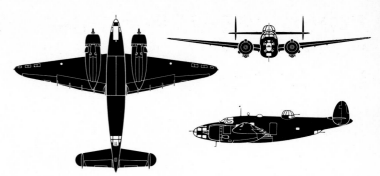

Origin: Vega Aircraft Corporation, Burbank, California.
Type: Bomber and reconnaissance aircraft.
Engines: Two Pratt & Whitney R-2800 Double Wasp 18-cylinder radials, (Ventura I) 1,850hp R-2800-S1A4-G, (most others) 2,000hp R-2800-31.
Dimensions: Span 65ft 6in (19·96m), (H) 75ft 0in (22·86m); length 51ft 5in to 51ft 9in (15·77m); height 13ft 2in to 14ft 1in (4·29m).
Weights: Empty (PV-1, typical) 19,373lb (8788kg), (H) about 24,000lb (10,886kg); maximum (V) 31,077lb (14,097kg), (H) 40,000lb (18,144kg).
Performance: Maximum speed (V) 300mph (483km/h), (H) 282mph (454km/h); maximum range with max bomb load (all) about 900 miles (1448km).
Armament: See text.
History: First flight (RAF) 31 July 1941; service delivery (RAF) June 1942; final delivery (H) 1945.
Users: (WWII) Australia, Italy (CB), New Zealand, Portugal, South Africa, UK (RAF), US (AAF, Navy).

Above: Three-view of all Venturas (B-34 similar).

Development: Vega Aircraft, a 1940 subsidiary of Lockheed, was awarded a contract by the British Purchasing Commission in June 1940 for 875 of a new design of bomber derived from the Lockheed 18 airliner. Called Lockheed V-146, or Vega 37, it resembled a more powerful Hudson, with longer fuselage provided with a rear ventral position with two 0·303in Brownings. Two (later four) more were in the dorsal turret, and the nose had two fixed 0·5in and two manually aimed 0·303in. Bomb load was 2,500lb (1134kg). In October 1942 Bomber Command's No 21 Sqn swept into action with a gallant daylight attack on the Phillips works at Eindhoven, but the Ventura proved a mediocre bomber and deliveries stopped at about 300. The B-34 Lexington absorbed many of the unwanted machines, though the Army Air Force never used them operationally. The B-34B trainer, Ventura II and IIA were reconnaissance models (originally O-56), but the bulk of the 1,600 Venturas were Navy PV-1 patrol bombers with up to eight 0·5in, more fuel and ability to carry mines and torpedoes. About 380 similar aircraft served Commonwealth forces as Ventura V, surviving in South Africa to the 1970s. The PV-2 Harpoon was redesigned as a much better Navy bomber, with larger wings, new tail and up to ten 0·5in, rockets and 4,000lb (1814kg) of bombs or torpedoes. The 535 built saw brief service before being passed to Allies.

Left: Swinging the compass of a white PV-1 of the US Navy. Many of these multi-role aircraft carried Mk IV ASV radar.

Martin 167 Maryland

Model 167 Maryland I and II

Origin: The Glenn L. Martin Company.
Type: Three-seat reconnaissance bomber.
Engines: Two Pratt & Whitney Twin Wasp 14-cylinder two-row radials; (Maryland I) 1,050hp R-1830-S1C3-G; (II) 1,200hp R-1830-S3C4-G.
Dimensions: Span 61ft 4in (18·69m); length 46ft 8in (14·22m); height 10ft 1in (3·07m).
Weights: Empty 11,213lb (RAF Mk II); maximum loaded (I) 15,297lb; (II) 16,809lb (7694kg).
Performance: Maximum speed (prototype) 316mph; (I) 304mph; (II) 280mph (451km/h); initial climb 1,790ft (545m)/min; service ceiling (I) 29,500ft (8992m); (II) 26,000ft (7925m); range with bomb load 1,080 miles (1738km).
Armament: Four 0·303in Browning (France, 7·5mm MAC 1934) fixed in outer wings, two 0·303in Vickers K (France, MAC 1934) manually aimed from dorsal turret and rear ventral position; internal bomb load of 2,000lb (907kg) (France 1,874lb, 850kg; Maryland I 1,250lb, 567kg).
History: First flight 14 March 1939; (production 167F) 7 August 1939; service delivery (France) October 1939; final delivery 1941.
Users: France, South Africa, UK (RAF, RN).

Development: Designed as the US Army XA-22 attack bomber, the Martin 167 was not adopted but immediately attracted a big French order for the Armée de l'Air as the 167F, with Armée de l'Air designation 167A-3. Of 215 purchased, about 75 reached France before the June 1940 capitulation, squadrons GB I/62 and I/63 completing conversion and, despite being chosen for dangerous missions, suffering only 8 per cent casualties (the lowest of any French bomber type). Some survivors and undelivered aircraft went to the RAF, while most surviving French aircraft served the Vichy Air Force and operated against the Allies over Gibraltar, North Africa and Syria. The RAF accepted 75 ex-French machines and bought a further 150 with two-stage supercharged engines as the Maryland II, using all 225 as reconnaissance bombers in Cyrenaica, Malta and other Middle East areas. A few went to the Fleet Air Arm (one gave first warning of the departure of *Bismarck*) and four squadrons served with the South African AF. In basic arrangement rather like Luftwaffe bombers, the Maryland was quite fast, nice to fly, but cramped and inadequately armed.

Below: Martin 167A-3 of GB I/63, Armée de l'Air.

Below: AR702 was the first Maryland to be supplied to the RAF. Built to US standards, with single-stage Twin Wasps, this batch was ordered by France.

Martin 179 B-26 Marauder

Model 179, B-26A to G, Marauder I to III

Origin: The Glenn L. Martin Company.

Type: Five- to seven-seat medium bomber.

Engines: Two Pratt & Whitney Double Wasp 18-cylinder two-row radials; (B-26) 1,850hp R-2800-5; (A) 2,000hp R-2800-39; (B, C, D, E, F, G) 2,000hp R-2800-43.

Dimensions: Span (B-26, A and first 641 B-26B) 65ft (19·8m); (remainder) 71ft (21·64m); length (B-26) 56ft, (A, B) 58ft 3in (17·75m); (F, G) 56ft 6in (17·23m); height (up to E) 19ft 10in (6·04m); (remainder) 21ft 6in (6·55m).

Weights: Empty (early, typical) 23,000lb (10,433kg); (F, G) 25,300lb (11,490kg); maximum loaded (B-26) 32,000lb; (A) 33,022lb; (first 641 B) 34,000lb, then 37,000lb (16,783kg); (F) 38,000lb (G) 38,200lb (17,340kg).

Performance: Maximum speed (up to E, typical) 310mph (500km/h); (F, G) 280mph (451km/h); initial climb 1,000ft (305m)/min; service ceiling (up to E) 23,000ft (7000m); (F, G) 19,800ft (6040m); range with 3,000lb (1361kg) bomb load (typical) 1,150 miles (1850km).

Armament: (B-26, A) five 0·30in or 0·50in Browning in nose (1 or 2), power dorsal turret (2), tail (1, manual) and optional manual ventral hatch; (B to E) one 0·5in manually aimed in nose, twin-gun turret, two manually aimed 0·5in waist guns, one "tunnel gun" (usually 0·5in), two 0·5in in power tail turret and four 0·5in fixed as "package guns" on sides of forward fuselage; (F, G) same but without tunnel gun; some variations and trainer and Navy versions unarmed. Internal bomb load of 5,200lb (2359kg) up to 641st B, after which rear bay was disused (eliminated in F, G) to give maximum load of 4,000lb (1814kg). Early versions could carry two torpedoes.

History: First flight 25 November 1940; service delivery 25 February 1941; final delivery March 1945.

Users: France, South Africa, UK (RAF), US (AAF, Navy).

Development: With its background of leadership in bomber design, Martin pulled out all the stops to win the 1939 Medium Bomber competition of the US Army, and boldly chose a wing optimised for high-speed cruise efficiency rather than for landing. Though the Model 179 won the competition — 201 being ordered "off the drawing board" on 5 July 1939 — the actual hardware proved too much for inexperienced pilots to handle, with unprecedented wing loading. In fact there were no real problems, but the newness of the first B-26 versions, coupled with their reputation of being a

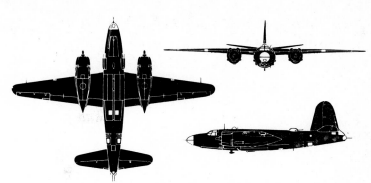

Above: Three-view of B-26C (Marauder III similar).

"widow maker", created a vicious circle of high casualties. Production B-26A models, with torpedo shackles between the bomb doors, were deployed to Australia the day after Pearl Harbor (8 December 1941), and later B models saw extensive South West Pacific service with the rear bomb bay used as a fuel tank (maximum bomb load 2,000lb). From the 641st B the wing and vertical tail were extended and on 14 May 1943 the Marauder began its career as the chief medium bomber of the 9th AF in the ETO (European Theatre of Operations). By VE-day the B-26 had set a record for the lowest loss-rate of any US Army bomber in Europe. About 522 also served with the RAF and South African AF in Italy. Total production amounted to 5,157 for the US Army (including Allied forces) plus a few dozen JM-1 and -2 target tug, reconnaissance and utility versions for the US Navy and about 200 AT-23 (later called TB-26) trainers. In 1948 the Marauder was withdrawn, and the B-26 designation passed to the Douglas Invader.

Right: This chrome-yellow beast is one of the early JM-1 target-towing and utility versions converted by the US Navy from early short-span bombers (pre-B-26B-10 block numbers). The Army Air Force counterpart was the TB-26B. The JM-1P was a photographic reconnaissance version.

Right: By far the most important user of the B-26 Marauder was the US 9th Army Air Force in the European theatre of operations. The aircraft illustrated was a B-26B-55 assigned to the 9th AAF 397th Bombardment Group (note invasion stripes).

Below: Students of the B-26 will know which outfit operated "Clark's Little Pill", leading a stream of C-models round a British taxiway. Tail numbers suggest the 323rd or 386th Bomb Groups of the 8th (not 9th) AAF.

Martin 187 Baltimore

Model 187, Baltimore I to V
(US Army A-30)

Origin: The Glenn L. Martin Company.
Type: Four-seat light bomber.
Engines: Two Wright Cyclone 14-cylinder two-row radials; (I, II) 1,600hp R-2600-A5B; (III, IV) 1,660hp R-2600-19; (V) 1,700hp R-2600-29.
Dimensions: Span 61ft 4in (18·69m); length 48ft 6in (14·78m); height 17ft 9in (5·41m).
Weights: Empty (III) 15,200lb (6895kg); maximum loaded (I) 22,958lb; (III) 23,000lb (10,433kg); (V) 27,850lb (12,632kg).
Performance: Maximum speed (I) 308mph; (III, IV) 302mph; (V) 320mph (515km/h); initial climb 1,500ft (457m)/min; service ceiling (typical) 24,000ft (7315m); range with 1,000lb bomb load (typical) 1,060 miles (1700km).
Armament: Four 0·303in Brownings fixed in outer wings; mid-upper position with manually aimed 0·303in Vickers K (I), twin Vickers (II), Boulton Paul turret with two or four 0·303in Browning (III), Martin turret with two 0·5in Browning (IV, V); rear ventral position with two 0·303in Vickers K; optional four or six fixed 0·303in guns firing directly to rear or obliquely downward. Internal bomb load up to 2,000lb (907kg).
History: First flight 14 June 1941; service delivery October 1941; final delivery May 1944.
Users: Australia, France, Italy, South Africa, Turkey, UK (RAF, RN).

Development: Martin received an RAF order in May 1940 for 400 improved Maryland bombers with deeper fuselages to allow intercommunication between crew members. In the course of design the more powerful R-2600 engine was adopted and the final aircraft marked an appreciable all-round improvement. The 400 were made up of 50 Mk I, 100 Mk II and 250 Mk III differing mainly in mid-upper armament. To facilitate Lend-Lease contracts, under which additional machines were ordered, the Model 187 was given the US Army designation A-30, but none were supplied for American use. After 281 Mk IIIA, identical to the III but on

Above: Ex-RAF Baltimore IV bombers flying over the Balkans with the Stormo Baltimore of the Italian Co-Belligerent AF. Seldom hitting the headlines, the Baltimore earned its keep.

US Lend-Lease account, and 294 Mk IV, production completed with 600 Mk V (A-30A), the total being 1,575 all for the RAF. Many were passed on to the South African AF, and a few to the Royal Navy, all being worked very hard in Cyrenaica, Tunisia, Sicily and Italy in bombing and close-support missions. In 1944 units of the co-belligerent Italian forces received ex-RAF machines and formed the Stormo Baltimore which was active over Jugoslavia and the Balkans.

Martin 162 PBM Mariner

Model 162, PBM-1 to 5A, Mariner GR.I

Origin: The Glenn L. Martin Company.
Type: Maritime patrol and anti-submarine flying boat with typical crew of nine.
Engines: (PBM-1) two 1,600hp Wright R-2600-6 Double Cyclone 14-cylinder two-row radials; (3C, 3S, 3R) 1,700hp R-2600-12; (3D) 1,900hp R-2600-22, (5, 5A) 2,100hp Pratt & Whitney R-2800-34 Double Wasp 18-cylinder two-row radials.
Dimensions: Span 118ft (36m); length (-1, 3S) 77ft 2in (23·5m); (3C) 80ft (24·38m); (5, 5A) 79ft 10in; height (-1) 24ft 6in; (remainder) 27ft 6in (8·4m).
Weights: Empty (-1) 26,600lb; (-3, typical) 32,328lb (14,690kg); (-5A)

34,000lb (15,422kg); maximum loaded (-1) 41,139lb; (3S) 56,000lb (25,400kg); (5) 60,000lb (27,216kg).
Performance: Maximum speed (all) about 205mph (330km/h); initial climb (typical) 800ft (244m)/min; service ceiling (-1) 22,400ft; (3S) 16,900ft; (5) 20,200ft (6160m); maximum range with military load (-1) 3,450 miles; (3C) 2,137 miles; (3S) 3,000 miles (4828km); (5) 2,700 miles (4345km).
Armament: (-1) one 0·5in Browning in nose turret, two in dorsal turret and two manually aimed from waist windows, one 0·30in in extreme tail (manually aimed over small cone of fire); (3B, 3C) twin-0·5in dorsal, nose and tail turrets; (3S) four manually aimed 0·5in in nose, tail and two waist windows; (5) eight 0·5in in three power turrets and two waist windows; weapon bays in engine nacelles with capacity of 2,000lb (907kg) in (-1) 4,000lb (1814kg) in all later versions (with provision for two externally hung torpedoes).
History: First flight (XPBM-1) 18 February 1939; service delivery (-1) September 1940; first flight (-5) May 1943; final delivery (5A) April 1949.
Users: Brazil, UK (RAF), US (Navy).

Development: Had it not been for the Catalina the PBM would have been by far the most important Allied patrol flying boat of World War II. It was designed in 1936 and proved by flying a quarter-scale model (Martin 162A). The full-size prototype was ordered on 3 June 1937, followed by 20 production -1 in December 1937. These were advanced and challenging boats, with high wing and power loading and stabilising floats which retracted inwards into the wing. Only one XPBM-2 was built, with long-range tanks and stressed for catapulting. Hundreds followed of the -3, -3C (which sank the U-boat which sank *Ark Royal*), -3R transport and -3S long-range anti-submarine versions, followed by the turreted -3D used throughout the South West Pacific. A small number of -3B served with RAF Coastal Command in 1943. The more powerful -5 had improved dorsal ASV radar (usually APS-15), the -5A was an amphibian and the post-war 5E had later equipment. Total deliveries were 1,235, and over 500 were in front-line service in the Korean war in 1950–53.

Left: This PBM-3S has two manually-aimed 0·5in nose guns and the usual search radar. All turrets were omitted from this ASW version.

Below: The PBM-5 was the last major production version, with powerful Double Wasp engines.

Martin 123, 139 and 166 Bomber

Model 123, 139 and 166, B-10, -12 and -14

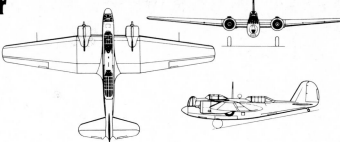

Origin: The Glenn L. Martin Company.
Type: 4/5-seat medium bomber.
Engines: (YB-10) two 775hp Wright R-1820-25 Cyclone nine-cylinder radials; (YB-12) two 665hp Pratt & Whitney R-1690-11 Hornet nine-cylinder radials; (XB-14) two 850hp P&W R-1830-9 Twin Wasp 14-cylinder two-row radials; (most export 139) 750hp Cyclone SGR-1820-F3S; (export 166) usually 850hp Cyclone R-1820-G2, but some 900hp Twin Wasp R-1830-SC3-G.
Dimensions: Span 70ft 6in (21·48m); length 44ft 8⅔in (13·63m); (XB-10) 45ft; (B-12A) 45ft 3in; (export 166) 44ft 2in; height 11ft (3·35m); (XB-10) 10ft 4in; (B-10B) 15ft 5in; (export 166) 11ft 7in.
Weights: Empty (typical B-10, 139) 8,870–9,000lb; (166) 10,900lb (4944kg); maximum loaded (XB-10) 12,560lb; (B-10B) 14,600lb (6622kg); (B-12A) 14,200lb; (139) 14,192lb; (166) 15,624lb (Cyclone) or 16,100lb (Twin Wasp).
Performance: Maximum speed (all B-10, 139, B-12) 207–213mph (340km/h); (166) 255mph (W) or 268mph (P&W); initial climb (all) 1,290–1,455ft (about 410m)/min; service ceiling (all) 24,200–25,200ft (about 500m); range with bomb load (typical) 700 miles (1125km); maximum range with extra fuel (early models) 1,240 miles, (166) 2,080 miles.
Armament: (All) three rifle-calibre (usually 0·3in) machine guns manually aimed from nose turret, rear cockpit and rear ventral hatch; bomb load of 1,000lb (454kg) in internal bay beneath centre section in fuselage.
History: First flight (Model 123) January 1932; service delivery (123) 20 March 1932; (YB-10) June 1934; (export 139) late 1935; (166) January 1938.
Users: (WWII) Argentina, Netherlands East Indies, Turkey.

Development: The Glenn L. Martin Company, of Baltimore, was one of the earliest important suppliers of US Army and Navy aircraft, and "Billy" Mitchell used Martin MB-2 bombers to demonstrate, in 1922, that battle-

Above: Three-view of Martin B-10B (except for Model 166, others similar apart from engine installations).

ships could be sunk from the air. After many historic heavy bombers, torpedo bombers, dive bombers and flying boats, Martin built the Model 123 as a company venture. Several recent observers have judged "the Martin Bomber" one of the most significant single advances in the history of military aircraft. For the first time it introduced cantilever monoplane wings, flaps, stressed-skin construction, retractable landing gear, advanced engine cowls, variable-pitch propellers and an internal bomb bay with power-driven doors. Despite only 600hp Cyclone engines the prototype walked away from every pursuit (fighter) in the US Army and the Model 139 went into production as the YB-10, followed by the 12 and 14, total delivery being 152 by 1936. Export sales were inevitable and once these were permitted, in 1935, a further 189 were built. By far the largest user was the Dutch East Indies, which bought 120 Martin 139W and 18 of the improved 166 with single "glasshouse" canopy. All the Netherlands Indies machines were in constant action from December 1941 as the only bombers available until late January 1942, fighting fiercely and with much success against Japanese sea and land forces. Other major users were Argentina (25) and Turkey (20).

Right: A Martin 139W-H2 exported to the Netherlands East Indies and used by the Luchtvaartdienst Army Air Division. A total of 117 of these bombers were bought by that service, and though obsolescent when the Japanese attacked in December 1941 they fought courageously. Most were of a slightly later design with long "greenhouse" canopy.

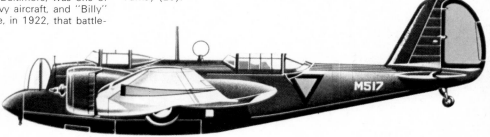

North American NA-16 (T-6 Texan, Harvard) family

AT-6/BC-1/SNJ series (Texan) and Harvard; (data for post-war T-6G)

Origin: North American Aviation Inc, Inglewood, Downey and Dallas; built under licence by Noorduyn Aviation and (post-war) Canadian Car & Foundry, Canada; Commonwealth Aircraft Corporation, Australia; ASJA (later Saab), Sweden; KK Watanabe and Nippon Hikoki KK, Japan; and Construcoes Aeronauticas SA, Brazil.
Type: Two-seat (some, single-seat) basic or advanced trainer, and attack.
Engine: Typically one 550hp Pratt & Whitney R-1340-AN1 nine-cylinder radial (see text).
Dimensions: Span 42ft 0¼in (12·8m); length 29ft 6in (8·99m); height 11ft 8½in (3·56m).
Weights: Empty 4,271lb (1938kg); loaded 5,617lb (2546kg).
Performance: Maximum speed 212mph (341km/h); initial climb 1,640ft (500m)/min; service ceiling 24,750ft (7338m); range 870 miles (1400km);
Armament: Normally provision for machine gun in either or both wing

roots and manually aimed in rear cockpit; light series wing bomb racks.
History: First flight (NA-16 prototype) April 1935; (production BT-9) April 1936; (NA-26) 1937; (Wirraway) 27 March 1939.
Users: (Wartime) Argentina, Australia, Bolivia, Brazil, Chile, China, Colombia, Cuba, Dominica, Ecuador, France, Honduras, Italy (Co-Belligerent), Japan, Mexico, Netherlands, New Zealand, Paraguay, South Africa, Southern Rhodesia, Soviet Union, Sweden, UK, USA (AAC/AAF, Navy, Marines), Uruguay, Venezuela.

Development: Perhaps the most varied family of aircraft in history began as a little monoplane trainer, with fixed gear and two open cockpits but all-metal stressed-skin construction, flown as a US civil machine in 1935. Its first offspring was the BT-9 basic trainer, supplied to many countries and made in many more (Yale was the RCAF name), powered by Wright R-975 Whirlwind, P&W Wasp Junior or Wasp engine. About 970 were built by North American. A second family were combat warplanes. Biggest family were the T-6 Harvard/Texan trainers derived from the NA-26, of which 15,109 were made by NAA in 1938–45, 755 in Australia as CAC Wirraways, 2,610 by Noorduyn in Canada, 176 by Japan (even receiving an Allied code-name: "Oak") and 136 by Saab in Sweden. By far the most important Allied training machine in World War II, thousands were re-furbished or remanufactured (2,068 by the original maker) in 1946–59 for 54 nations. Cancar built 555 T-6G in 1951–54.

Left: A large group of Harvard IIAs, from a training school in Canada. The IIA was a mass-produced version containing almost no aluminium alloys, steel and wood taking their place. Later came the AT-6D (Harvard III) with the original structure.

Below: The original Harvard I, as introduced to the RAF at Grantham in December 1938.

North American NA-62 B-25 Mitchell

B-25 to TB-25N, PBJ series, F-10

Origin: North American Aviation Inc, Inglewood and Kansas City.
Type: Medium bomber and attack with crew from four to six (see text).
Engines: (B-25, A, B), two 1,700hp Wright R-2600-9 Double Cyclone 14-cylinder two-row radials; (C, D, G) two 1,700hp R-2600-13; (H, J, F-10), two 1,850hp (emergency rating) R-2600-29.
Dimensions: Span 67ft 7in (20·6m); length (B-25, A) 54ft 1in; (B, C, J) 52ft 11in (16·1m); (G, H) 51ft (15·54m); height (typical) 15ft 9in (4·80m).
Weights: Empty (J, typical) 21,100lb (9580kg); maximum loaded (A) 27,100lb; (B) 28,640lb; (C) 34,000lb (15,422kg); (G) 35,000lb (15,876kg); (H) 36,047lb (16,350kg); (J) normal 35,000lb, overload 41,800lb (18,960 kg).
Performance: Maximum speed (A) 315mph; (B) 300mph; (C, G) 284mph (459km/h); (H, J) 275mph (443km/h); initial climb (A, typical) 1,500ft (460m)/min; (late models, typical) 1,100ft (338m)/min; service ceiling (A) 27,000ft (8230m); (late models, typical) 24,000ft (7315m); range (all, typical) 1,500 miles (2414km).
Armament: See text.
History: First flight (NA-40 prototype) January 1939; (NA-62, the first production B-25) 19 August 1940; (B-25G) August 1942.
Users: (Wartime) Australia, Brazil, China, France (FFL), Italy (Co-Belligerent), Mexico, Netherlands (1944), Soviet Union, UK (RAF, RN), US (AAC/AAF, Navy).

Development: Named in honour of the fearless US Army Air Corps officer who was court-martialled in 1924 for his tiresome (to officialdom) belief in air power, the B-25 — designed by a company with no previous experience of twins, of bombers or of high performance warplanes — was made in larger quantities than any other American twin-engined combat

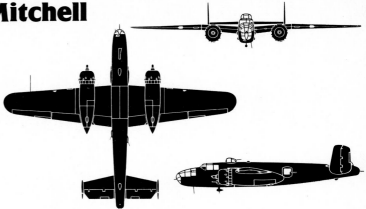

Above: Three-view of B-25J (RAF, Mitchell III).

aircraft and has often been described as the best aircraft in its class in World War II. Led by Lee Atwood and Ray Rice, the design team first created the Twin Wasp-powered NA-40, but had to start again and build a sleeker and more powerful machine to meet revised Army specifications demanding twice the bomb load (2,400lb, 1089kg). The Army ordered 184 off the drawing board, the first 24 being B-25s and the rest B-25A with armour and self-sealing tanks. The defensive armament was a 0·5in manually aimed in the cramped tail and single 0·3in manually aimed from waist windows and the nose; bomb load was 3,000lb (1361kg). The B had twin 0·5in in an electrically driven dorsal turret and a retractable ventral turret, the tail gun being removed. On 18 April 1942 16 B-25Bs led by Lt-Col Jimmy Doolittle made the daring and morale-raising raid on Tokyo, having made free take-offs at gross weight from the carrier *Hornet* 800 miles distant. Extra fuel, external bomb racks and other additions led to the C, supplied to the RAF, China and Soviet Union, and as PBJ-1C to the US Navy. The D was similar but built at the new plant at Kansas City. In 1942 came the G, with solid nose fitted with a 75mm M-4 gun, loaded manually with 21 rounds. At first two 0·5in were also fixed in the nose, for flak suppression and sighting, but in July 1943 tests against Japanese ships showed that more was needed and the answer was four 0·5in "package guns" on the sides of the nose. Next came the B-25H with the fearsome armament of a 75mm, 14 0·5in guns (eight firing ahead, two in waist bulges and four in dorsal and tail turrets) and a 2,000lb (907kg) torpedo or 3,200lb (1451kg) of bombs. Biggest production of all was of the J, with glazed nose, normal bomb load of 4,000lb (1814kg) and 13 0·5in guns supplied with 5,000 rounds. The corresponding attack version had a solid nose with five additional 0·5in guns. Total J output was 4,318, and the last delivery in August 1945 brought total output to 9,816. The F-10 was an unarmed multi-camera reconnaissance version, and the CB-25 was a post-war transport model. The wartime AT-24 trainers were redesignated TB-25 and, after 1947, supplemented by more than 900 bombers rebuilt as the TB-25J, K, L and M. Many ended their days as research hacks or target tugs and one carried the cameras for the early Cinerama films.

Above: First model with the slow-firing but punchy 75mm gun was the B-25G. Then came the hard-hitting B-25H, see text.

Below: This B-25J was one of 870 of various sub-types supplied freely under Lend-Lease to the Soviet Union in 1941-44.

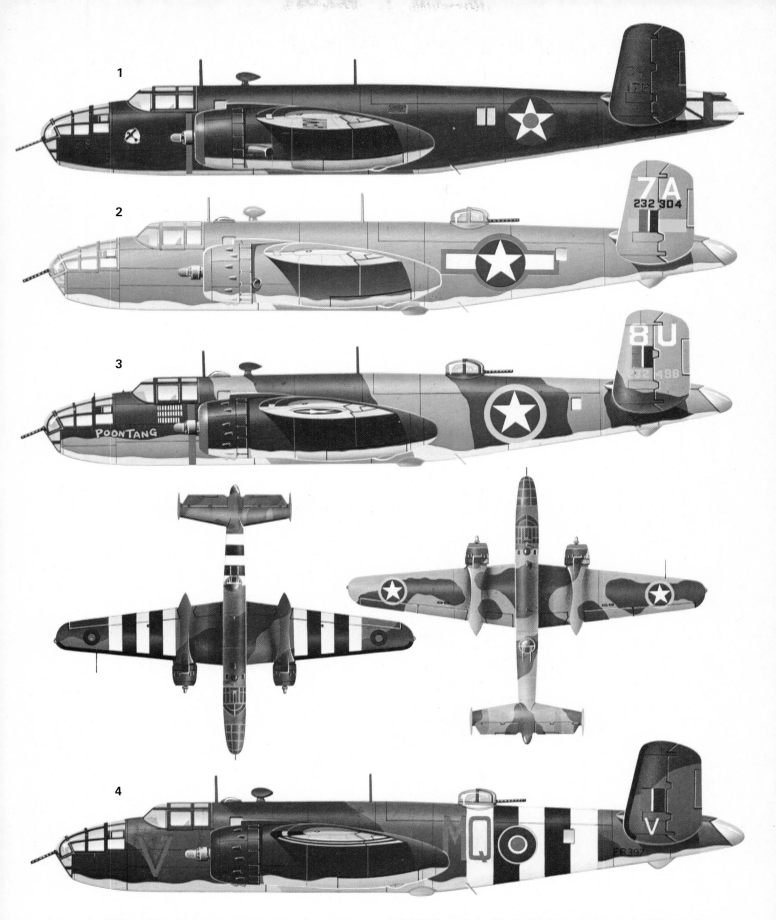

Above: The early B-25A with its single manually-aimed nose and tail machine guns soon gave way to the B-25B, with powered dorsal turret and retractable ventral turret, and the similarly armed C and D (designated Mitchell II in RAF service). Later models of the Mitchell, which was built in greater numbers than any other twin-engined American combat aircraft, featured still heavier armament, and the type's overall record on every battlefront of the war established it as one of the most successful aircraft of its class.

1: B-25A serving with the 34th Bomb Squadron, 17th Bomb Group, at Pendleton, Oregon, in September 1941.

2: B-25C-10 serving with the 487th Bomb Squadron, 340th Bomb Group, based at Catania, Sicily, in September 1943. The paint scheme is Desert Sand on the upper surfaces and Sky Blue on the undersides.

3: B-25C-15 of the 488th Bomb Squadron, 340th Bomb Group, at Sfax, Tunisia, in April 1943, and (below right) upper surfaces of the same aircraft, with olive drab disruptive pattern over the Desert Sand.

4: RAF Mitchell II serving with 226 Squadron, 2nd Tactical Air Force during operations from Gilze Rijen, Netherlands, in June 1945; wing (above left) and fuselage invasion stripes are still in evidence.

North American NA-73 P-51/A-36 Mustang

P-51 to P-51L, A-36, F-6, Cavalier 750 to 2500, Piper Enforcer and F-82 Twin Mustang

Origin: North American Aviation Inc, Inglewood and Dallas; built under licence by Commonwealth Aircraft Corporation, Australia (and post-war by Cavalier and Piper).

Type: (P-51) single-seat fighter; (A-36) attack bomber; (F-6) reconnaissance; (post-war Cavalier and Piper models) Co-In; (F-82) night fighter.

Engine: (P-51, A, A-36, F-6A) one 1,150hp Allison V-1710-F3R or 1,125hp V-1710-81 vee-12 liquid-cooled; (P-51B, C, D and K, F-6C) one Packard V-1650 (licence-built R-R Merlin 61-series), originally 1,520hp V-1650-3 followed during P-51D run by 1,590hp V-1650-7; (P-51H) 2,218hp V-1650-9; (Cavalier) mainly V-1650-7; (Turbo-Mustang III) 1,740hp Rolls-Royce Dart 510 turboprop; (Enforcer) 2,535hp Lycoming T55-9 turboprop; (F-82F, G, H) two 2,300hp (wet rating) Allison V-1710-143/145.

Dimensions: Span 37ft 0½in (11·29m); (F-82) 51ft 3in (15·61m); length 32ft 2½in (9·81m); (P-51H) 33ft 4in; (F-82E) 39ft 1in (11·88m); height (P-51, A, A-36, F-6) 12ft 2in (3·72m); (other P-51) 13ft 8in (4·1m); (F-82) 13ft 10in (4·2m).

Weights: Empty (P-51 early V-1710 models, typical) 6,300lb (2858kg); (P-51D) 7,125lb (3230kg); (F-82E) 14,350lb (6509kg); maximum loaded (P-51 early) 8,600lb (3901kg); (P-51D) 11,600lb (5,206kg); (F-82E) 24,864lb (11,276kg).

Performance: Maximum speed (early P-51) 390mph (628km/h); (P-51D) 437mph (703km/h); (F-82, typical) 465mph (750km/h); initial climb (early) 2,600ft (792m)/min, (P-51D) 3,475ft (1060m)/min; service ceiling (early) 30,000ft (9144m); (P-51D) 41,900ft (12,770m), range with maximum fuel (early) 450 miles (724km); (P-51D) combat range 950 miles, operational range 1,300 miles with drop tanks and absolute range to dry tanks of 2,080 miles; (F-82E) 2,504 miles.

North American P-51 Mustang cutaway drawing key:

1 Plastic (Phenol fibre) rudder trim tab
2 Rudder frame (fabric covered)
3 Rudder balance
4 Fin front spar
5 Fin structure
6 Access panel
7 Rudder trim-tab actuating drum
8 Rudder trim-tab control link
9 Rear navigation light
10 Rudder metal bottom section
11 Elevator plywood trim tab
12 Starboard elevator frame
13 Elevator balance weight
14 Starboard tailplane structure
15 Reinforced bracket (rear steering stresses)
16 Rudder operating horn forging
17 Elevator operating horns
18 Tab control turnbuckles
19 Fin front spar/fuselage attachment
20 Port elevator tab
21 Fabric-covered elevator
22 Elevator balance weight
23 Port tailplane
24 Tab control drum
25 Fin root fairing
26 Elevator cables
27 Tab control access panels
28 Tailwheel steering mechanism
29 Tailwheel retraction mechanism
30 Tailwheel leg assembly
31 Forward-retracting steerable tailwheel
32 Tailwheel doors
33 Lifting tube
34 Fuselage aft bulkhead/ break point
35 Fuselage break point
36 Control cable pulley brackets
37 Fuselage frames
38 Oxygen bottles
39 Cooling-air exit flap actuating mechanism
40 Rudder cables
41 Fuselage lower longeron
42 Rear tunnel
43 Cooling-air exit flap
44 Coolant radiator assembly
45 Radio and equipment shelf
46 Power supply pack
47 Fuselage upper longeron
48 Radio bay aft bulkhead (plywood)

49 Fuselage stringers
50 SCR-695 radio transmitter-receiver (on upper sliding shelf)
51 Whip aerial
52 Junction box
53 Cockpit aft glazing
54 Canopy track
55 SCR-522 radio transmitter-receiver
56 Battery installation
57 Radiator/supercharger coolant pipes
58 Radiator forward air duct
59 Coolant header tank/radiator pipe
60 Coolant radiator ventral access cover
61 Oil-cooler air inlet door
62 Oil radiator
63 Oil pipes
64 Flap control linkage
65 Wing rear spar/fuselage attachment bracket
66 Crash pylon structure
67 Aileron control linkage
68 Hydraulic hand pump
69 Radio control boxes
70 Pilot's seat
71 Seat suspension frame
72 Pilot's head/back armour
73 Rearward-sliding clear-vision canopy
74 External rear-view mirror
75 Ring and bead gunsight
76 Bullet-proof windshield
77 Gyro gunsight
78 Engine controls
79 Signal-pistol discharge tube
80 Circuit-breaker panel
81 Oxygen regulator
82 Pilot's footrest and seat mounting bracket
83 Control linkage
84 Rudder pedal
85 Tailwheel lock control
86 Wing centre-section
87 Hydraulic reservoir
88 Port wing fuel tank filler point
89 Port Browning 0·5in guns
90 Ammunition feed chutes
91 Gun-bay access door (raised)
92 Ammunition box troughs
93 Aileron control cables
94 Flap lower skin (Alclad)
95 Aileron profile (internal aerodynamic balance diaphragm)

96 Aileron control drum and mounting bracket
97 Aileron trim-tab control drum
98 Aileron plastic (Phenol fibre) trim tab
99 Port aileron assembly
100 Wing skinning
101 Outer section sub-assembly
102 Port navigation light
103 Port wingtip
104 Leading-edge skin
105 Landing lamp
106 Weapons/stores pylon
107 500 lb (227 kg) bomb
108 Gun ports
109 Gun barrels
110 Detachable cowling panels
111 Firewall/integral armour
112 Oil tank
113 Oil pipes
114 Upper longeron/engine mount attachment
115 Oil-tank metal retaining straps
116 Carburettor
117 Engine bearer assembly
118 Cowling panel frames
119 Engine aftercooler
120 Engine leads
121 1,520 hp Packard V-1650 (R-R Merlin) twelve-cylinder liquid-cooled engine
122 Exhaust fairing panel
123 Stub exhausts
124 Magneto
125 Coolant pipes

52

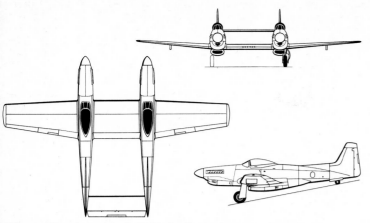

Above: The dramatic P-82 Twin Mustang was created very quickly in 1944, but did not see active service in World War II. Had it been started earlier it would have been a truly great war-winner.

Above: By mid-1944 the teardrop-canopy P-51D was numerically the most important fighter in the 8th Fighter Command in England. This one probably belonged to the 353rd FG, based at Raydon, with the checkerboard marking in black and yellow.

Left: The subject of the cutaway drawing is the P-51C. This was the interim sub-type with the V-1650 (Merlin) engine, a British-designed Malcolm bulged sliding canopy and other features not found in the P-51B, but the armament was still only four guns. In the meantime, North American Aviation had tested a beautiful streamlined bubble (teardrop) canopy on a modified P-51B with cut-down rear fuselage, and this led to the P-51D, with six guns.

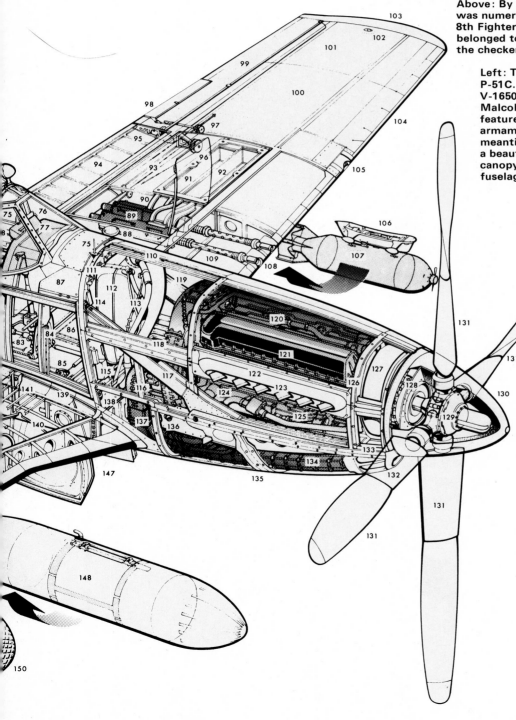

126 Cowling forward frame
127 Coolant header tank
128 Armour plate
129 Propeller hub
130 Spinner
131 Hamilton Standard Hydromatic propeller
132 Carburettor air intake, integral with (133)
133 Engine-mount front-frame assembly
134 Intake trunk
135 Engine-mount reinforcing tie
136 Hand-crank starter
137 Carburettor trunk vibration-absorbing connection
138 Wing centre-section front bulkhead
139 Wing centre-section end rib
140 Starboard mainwheel well
141 Wing front spar/fuselage attachment bracket
142 Ventral air intake (radiator and oil cooler)
143 Starboard wing fuel tank
144 Fuel filler point
145 Mainwheel leg mount/pivot
146 Mainwheel leg rib cut-outs
147 Main gear fairing doors
148 Auxiliary fuel tank (plastic/ pressed-paper composition, 90 gal/409 litres)
149 Auxiliary fuel tank (metal, 62·5 gal/284 litres)
150 27 in smooth-contour mainwheel
151 Axle fork
152 Towing lugs
153 Landing-gear fairing
154 Main-gear shock strut
155 Blast tubes
156 Wing front spar
157 Gun bay
158 Ammunition feed chutes
159 Ammunition boxes
160 Wing rear spar
161 Flap structure
162 Starboard aileron tab
163 Starboard aileron
164 Starboard aileron tab adjustment (ground setting)
165 Wing rib strengthening
166 Outboard section structure
167 Outer section single spar
168 Wingtip sub-assembly
169 Starboard navigation light
170 Detachable wingtip

►Armament: (RAF Mustang I) four 0·303in in wings, two 0·5in in wings and two 0·5in in lower sides of nose; (Mustang IA and P-51) four 20mm Hispano in wings; (P-51A and B) four 0·5in in wings; (A-36A) six 0·5in in wings and wing racks for two 500lb (227kg) bombs; (all subsequent P-51 production models) six 0·5in Browning MG53-2 with 270 or 400 rounds each, and wing racks for tanks or two 1,000lb (454kg) bombs; (F-82, typical) six 0·5in in centre wing, six or eight pylons for tanks, radars or up to 4,000lb weapons.

History: First flight (NA-73X) 26 October 1940; (production RAF Mustang I) 1 May 1941; service delivery (RAF) October 1941; first flight (Merlin conversion) 13 October 1942; (P-51B) December 1942; final delivery (P-51H) November 1945; first flight (XP-82A) 15 April 1945; final delivery (F-82G) April 1949.

Users: (Wartime) Australia, Canada, China (and AVG), Netherlands, New Zealand, Poland, South Africa, Soviet Union, Sweden, UK (RAF), USA (AAC/AAF).

Development: In April 1940 the British Air Purchasing Commission concluded with ''Dutch'' Kindelberger, chairman of North American Aviation, an agreement for the design and development of a completely new fighter for the RAF. Designed, built and flown in 117 days, this silver prototype was the start of the most successful fighter programme in history. The RAF received 620 Mustang I, 150 IA and 50 II, while the US Army adopted the type with 500 A-36A and 310 P-51A. In 1942 the brilliant airframe was matched with the Merlin engine, yielding the superb P-51B, bulged-hood C (Mustang III) and teardrop-canopy D (Mustang IV), later C and all D models having six 0·5in guns and a dorsal fin. The final models were the K (different propeller) and better-shaped, lighter H, the fastest of all at 487mph. Total production was 15,586. Mustang and P-51 variants served mainly in Europe, their prime mission being the almost incredible one of flying all the way from British bases to targets of the 8th AF deep in Germany — Berlin or beyond — escorting heavies and gradually establishing Allied air superiority over the heart of Germany. After the war the Mustang proved popular with at least 55 nations, while in 1947–49 the US Air Force bought 272 examples of the appreciably longer Twin Mustang (two Allison-powered fuselages on a common wing), most of them radar night fighters which served in Korea. In 1945–48 Commonwealth Aircraft of

Above: A swarm of P-51D Mustangs, each with two 91·6-gal drop tanks, giving a range in excess of 2,000 miles. These examples served with the 15th Air Force in northern Italy.

Australia made under licence 200 Mustangs of four versions. In 1967 the P-51 was put back into production by Cavalier for the US Air Force and other customers, and the turboprop Turbo III and Enforcer versions were developed for the Pave Coin programme for Forward Air Control and light attack missions. Many of the new or remanufactured models of 1968–75 are two-seaters.

Below: A fine picture of Mustangs of the 8th Air Force 361st Fighter Group, based at Bottisham but soon headed for a base in France (St Dizier). Furthest from the camera is a P-51B.

Above: The poor altitude performance of the original Allison-powered P-51A and A-36A for the USAAF and Mustang I, IA and II for the RAF was rectified by the substitution of a Merlin engine, and the resulting P-51B and C/Mustang III, along with subsequent models, established the type as one of the outstanding fighters of the war.

1: P-51B-5 "Shangri-La" flown by Capt Don S. Gentile of the 336th FS, 4th FG, Debden, March 1944, with the emblem of the group's 334th FS.

2: P-51B-10 "Shoo Shoo Baby", 364th FS, 357th FG, Leiston, spring 1944.

3: P-51B "Dorothy-II", serving with the 318th FS, 325th FG, in Italy late in 1944, and detail of the group's checkerboard tail markings.

4: P-51B-15 serving with the 374th FS, 361st FG, at Bottisham in June 1944, and detail of the D-Day invasion stripes worn by this aircraft.

5: Mustang IIIB in the markings of 316 (Polish) Squadron, RAF, based at Coltishall, in June 1944, also wearing invasion stripes.

6: Mustang III serving with 19 Squadron, RAF, at Ford in summer 1944.

Northrop P-61 Black Widow
P-61A, B and C and F-15 (RF-61C) Reporter

Origin: Northrop Aircraft Inc, Hawthorne, California.
Type: (P-61) three-seat night fighter; (F-15) two-seat strategic reconnaissance.
Engines: Two Pratt & Whitney R-2800 Double Wasp 18-cylinder two-row radials; (P-61A) 2,000hp R-2800-10; (B) 2,000hp R-2800-65; (C and F-15) 2,800hp (wet rating) R-2800-73.
Dimensions: Span 66ft (20·12m); length (A) 48ft 11in (14·92m); (B, C) 49ft 7in (15·1m); (F-15) 50ft 3in (15·3m); height (typical) 14ft 8in (4·49m).
Weights: Empty (typical P-61) 24,000lb (10,886kg); (F-15) 22,000lb (9979kg); maximum loaded (A) 32,400lb (14,696kg); (B) 38,000lb (17,237kg); (C) 40,300lb (18,280kg); (F-15, clean) 28,000lb (12,700kg).
Performance: maximum speed (A, B) 366mph (590km/h); (C) 430mph (692km/h); (F-15) 440mph (708km/h); initial climb (A, B) 2,200ft (670m)/min; (C, F-15) 3,000ft (914m)/min; service ceiling (A, B) 33,000ft (10,060m); (C, F-15) 41,000ft (12,500m); range with maximum fuel (A) 500 miles; (B, C) 2,800 miles (4500km); (F.15) 4,000 miles (6440km).

Above: Three-view of P-61A with turret (others similar).

Armament: Four Fixed 20mm M-2 cannon in belly, firing ahead (plus, in first 37 A, last 250 B and all C) electric dorsal turret with four 0·5in remotely controlled from front or rear sight station and fired by pilot; (B and C) underwing racks for 6,400lb load; (F-15A) no armament.
History: First flight (XP-61) 21 May 1942; service delivery (A) May 1944; first flight (F-15A) 1946.
User: USA (AAF).

Development: The first aircraft ever ordered to be designed explicitly as a night fighter, the XP-61 prototypes were ordered in January 1941 on the basis of combat reports from the early radar-equipped fighters of the RAF. A very big aircraft, the P-61 had the new SCR-720 AI radar in the nose, the armament being mounted well back above and below the rather lumpy nacelle housing pilot, radar operator and gunner with front and rear sighting stations. The broad wing had almost full-span double-slotted flaps, very small ailerons and lateral-control spoilers in an arrangement years ahead of its time. Black-painted (hence the name), the P-61A entered service with the 18th Fighter Group in the South Pacific and soon gained successes there and in Europe. Buffet from the turret led to this soon being deleted, but the B and C had pylons for the very heavy load of four 250 gal tanks or 6,400lb (2900kg) bombs. Total production was 941, followed by 35 slim photo-reconnaissance versions.

Left: Though one of the largest fighters of all time, the P-61 was surprisingly tractable, and its lateral controls (shown off in operation) were exciting.

Below: A P-61A-5, one of the first to reach Europe, with 422 NFS, 9th AAF, Scorton, England.

Below: Another turretless P-61A is seen here at readiness at a 9th AAF dispersal somewhere in England. D-day stripes were worn by all P-61s in the European theatre.

HUSSLIN HUSSEY   25536

Republic P-47 Thunderbolt

P-47B, C, D, M and N

Origin: Republic Aviation Corporation.
Type: Single-seat fighter; (D and N) fighter-bomber.
Engine: One Pratt & Whitney R-2800 Double Wasp 18-cylinder two-row radial; (B) 2,000hp R-2800-21; (C, most D) 2,300hp R-2800-59; (M, N) 2,800hp R-2800-57 or -77 (emergency wet rating).
Dimensions: Span 40ft 9¼in (12·4m); length (B) 34ft 10in; (C, D, M, N) 36ft 1¼in (11·03m); height (B) 12ft 8in; (C, D) 14ft 2in (4·3m); (M, N) 14ft 8in.
Weights: Empty (B) 9,010lb (4087kg); (D) 10,700lb (4853kg); maximum loaded (B) 12,700lb (5760kg); (C) 14,925lb; (D) 19,400lb (8800kg); (M) 14,700lb; (N) 21,200lb (9616kg).
Performance: Maximum speed (B) 412mph; (C) 433mph; (D) 428mph

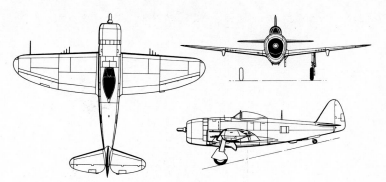

Above: Three view of P-47D-25.

(690km/h); (M) 470mph; (N) 467mph (751km/h); initial climb (typical) 2,800ft (855m)/min; service ceiling (B) 38,000ft; (C-N) 42,000—43,000ft (13,000m); range on internal fuel (B) 575 miles; (D) 1,000 miles (1600km); ultimate range (drop tanks) (D) 1,900 miles (3060km); (N) 2,350 miles (3800km).
Armament: (Except M) eight 0·5in Colt-Browning M-2 in wings, each with 267, 350 or 425 rounds (M) six 0·5in; (D and N) three to five racks for external load of tanks, bombs or rockets to maximum of 2,500lb (1134kg).
History: First flight (XP-47B) 6 May 1941; production delivery (B) 18 March 1942; final delivery (N) September 1945.
Users: Australia, Brazil, France, Soviet Union, UK (RAF), USA (AAF).

Development: Before the United States entered World War II it was eagerly digesting the results of air combats in Europe and, in 1940, existing plans by Republic's chief designer Alexander Kartveli were urgently replaced by sketches for a much bigger fighter with the new R-2800 engine. This appeared to be the only way to meet the Army Air Corps' new targets for fighter performance. Kartveli began by designing the best installation of the big engine and its turbocharger, placed under the rear fuselage. The air duct had to pass under the elliptical wing, and there were problems in achieving ground clearance for the big propeller (12ft diameter, even though it had the exceptional total of four blades) with landing gear able to retract inwards and still leave room in the wing for the formidable armament of eight 0·5in guns. After severe and protracted technical difficulties the P-47B was cleared for production in early 1942 and at the beginning of 1943 two fighter groups equipped with the giant new fighter (one the famed 56th, to become top scorers in Europe) joined the 8th AF in Britain to

Above: When first used in Europe the P-47B was given white stripes to distinguish it from a Focke-Wulf 190 (which it in no way resembled). This P-47D-10 is seen later with Group insignia, D-day stripes, 108-gal paper tank and two 500lb bombs.

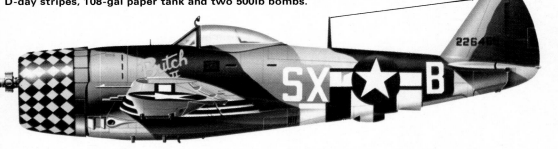

Left: Colourful P-47D-25 from the 352nd FS of the 353rd FG (same group that later used the P-51 on p. 243) based at Raydon.

Below: Early models became known as "razorbacks". These are probably over Long Island, but a yellow cowl would denote the 361st FG of the 8th AAF. The C introduced a longer fuselage and bomb/tank racks, the D a better engine, the D-25 the bubble hood and the D-30 a dorsal fin.

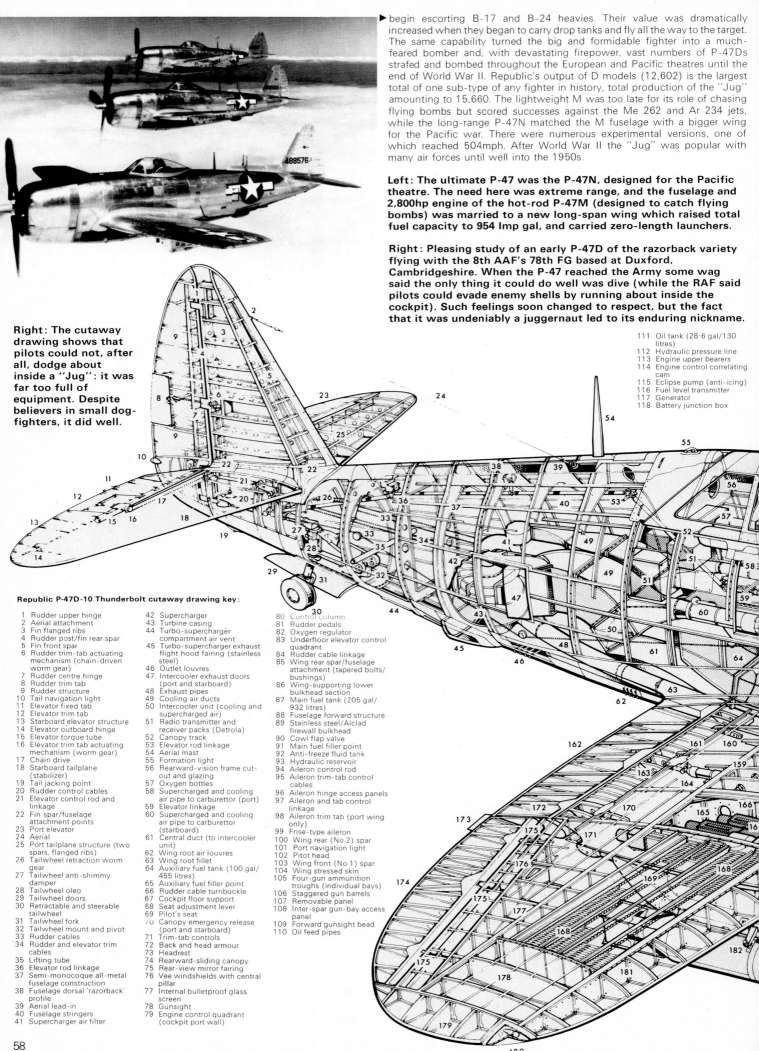

begin escorting B-17 and B-24 heavies. Their value was dramatically increased when they began to carry drop tanks and fly all the way to the target. The same capability turned the big and formidable fighter into a much-feared bomber and, with devastating firepower, vast numbers of P-47Ds strafed and bombed throughout the European and Pacific theatres until the end of World War II. Republic's output of D models (12,602) is the largest total of one sub-type of any fighter in history, total production of the "Jug" amounting to 15,660. The lightweight M was too late for its role of chasing flying bombs but scored successes against the Me 262 and Ar 234 jets, while the long-range P-47N matched the M fuselage with a bigger wing for the Pacific war. There were numerous experimental versions, one of which reached 504mph. After World War II the "Jug" was popular with many air forces until well into the 1950s.

Left: The ultimate P-47 was the P-47N, designed for the Pacific theatre. The need here was extreme range, and the fuselage and 2,800hp engine of the hot-rod P-47M (designed to catch flying bombs) was married to a new long-span wing which raised total fuel capacity to 954 Imp gal, and carried zero-length launchers.

Right: Pleasing study of an early P-47D of the razorback variety flying with the 8th AAF's 78th FG based at Duxford, Cambridgeshire. When the P-47 reached the Army some wag said the only thing it could do well was dive (while the RAF said pilots could evade enemy shells by running about inside the cockpit). Such feelings soon changed to respect, but the fact that it was undeniably a juggernaut led to its enduring nickname.

Right: The cutaway drawing shows that pilots could not, after all, dodge about inside a "Jug": it was far too full of equipment. Despite believers in small dog-fighters, it did well.

Republic P-47D-10 Thunderbolt cutaway drawing key:

1 Rudder upper hinge
2 Aerial attachment
3 Fin flanged ribs
4 Rudder post/fin rear spar
5 Fin front spar
6 Rudder trim-tab actuating mechanism (chain-driven worm gear)
7 Rudder centre hinge
8 Rudder trim tab
9 Rudder structure
10 Tail navigation light
11 Elevator fixed tab
12 Elevator trim tab
13 Starboard elevator structure
14 Elevator outboard hinge
15 Elevator torque tube
16 Elevator trim tab actuating mechanism (worm gear)
17 Chain drive
18 Starboard tailplane (stabilizer)
19 Tail jacking point
20 Rudder control cables
21 Elevator control rod and linkage
22 Fin spar/fuselage attachment points
23 Port elevator
24 Aerial
25 Port tailplane structure (two spars, flanged ribs)
26 Tailwheel retraction worm gear
27 Tailwheel anti-shimmy damper
28 Tailwheel oleo
29 Tailwheel doors
30 Retractable and steerable tailwheel
31 Tailwheel fork
32 Tailwheel mount and pivot
33 Rudder cables
34 Rudder and elevator trim cables
35 Lifting tube
36 Elevator rod linkage
37 Semi-monocoque all-metal fuselage construction
38 Fuselage dorsal 'razorback' profile
39 Aerial lead-in
40 Fuselage stringers
41 Supercharger air filter

42 Supercharger
43 Turbine casing
44 Turbo-supercharger compartment air vent
45 Turbo-supercharger exhaust flight hood fairing (stainless steel)
46 Outlet louvres
47 Intercooler exhaust doors (port and starboard)
48 Exhaust pipes
49 Cooling air ducts
50 Intercooler unit (cooling and supercharged air)
51 Radio transmitter and receiver packs (Detrola)
52 Canopy track
53 Elevator rod linkage
54 Aerial mast
55 Formation light
56 Rearward-vision frame cut-out and glazing
57 Oxygen bottles
58 Supercharged and cooling air pipe to carburettor (port)
59 Elevator linkage
60 Supercharged and cooling air pipe to carburettor (starboard)
61 Central duct (to intercooler unit)
62 Wing root air louvres
63 Wing root fillet
64 Auxiliary fuel tank (100 gal/455 litres)
65 Auxiliary fuel filler point
66 Rudder cable turnbuckle
67 Cockpit floor support
68 Seat adjustment lever
69 Pilot's seat
70 Canopy emergency release (port and starboard)
71 Trim-tab controls
72 Back and head armour
73 Headrest
74 Rearward-sliding canopy
75 Rear-view mirror fairing
76 Vee windshields with central pillar
77 Internal bulletproof glass screen
78 Gunsight
79 Engine control quadrant (cockpit port wall)

80 Control column
81 Rudder pedals
82 Oxygen regulator
83 Underfloor elevator control quadrant
84 Rudder cable linkage
85 Wing rear spar/fuselage attachment (tapered bolts/bushings)
86 Wing-supporting lower bulkhead section
87 Main fuel tank (205 gal/932 litres)
88 Fuselage forward structure
89 Stainless steel/Alclad firewall bulkhead
90 Cowl flap valve
91 Main fuel filler point
92 Anti-freeze fluid tank
93 Hydraulic reservoir
94 Aileron control rod
95 Aileron trim-tab control cables
96 Aileron hinge access panels
97 Aileron and tab control linkage
98 Aileron trim tab (port wing only)
99 Frise-type aileron
100 Wing rear (No 2) spar
101 Port navigation light
102 Pitot head
103 Wing front (No 1) spar
104 Wing stressed skin
105 Four-gun ammunition troughs (individual bays)
106 Staggered gun barrels
107 Removable panel
108 Inter-spar gun-bay access panel
109 Forward gunsight bead
110 Oil feed pipes

111 Oil tank (28·6 gal/130 litres)
112 Hydraulic pressure line
113 Engine upper bearers
114 Engine control correlating cam
115 Eclipse pump (anti-icing)
116 Fuel level transmitter
117 Generator
118 Battery junction box

119 Storage battery
120 Exhaust collector ring
121 Cowl flap actuating cylinder
122 Exhaust outlets to collector ring
123 Cowl flaps
124 Supercharged and cooling air ducts to carburettor (port and starboard)
125 Exhaust upper outlets
126 Cowling frame
127 2,000 hp Pratt & Whitney Double Wasp R-2800-21 eighteen-cylinder two-row engine
128 Cowling nose panel
129 Magnetos
130 Propeller governor
131 Propeller hub
132 Reduction gear casing
133 Spinner
134 Propeller cuffs
135 Curtiss constant-speed electric propeller (12 ft 2in)
136 Oil cooler intakes (port and starboard)
137 Supercharger intercooler (central) air intake
138 Ducting
139 Oil-cooler feed pipes
140 Starboard oil cooler
141 Engine lower bearers
142 Oil-cooler exhaust variable shutter
143 Fixed deflector
144 Excess exhaust gas gate
145 Belly stores/weapon shackles
146 Metal auxiliary drop tank (75 gal/341 litres)
147 Inboard mainwheel well door
148 Mainwheel well door actuating cylinder
149 Camera gun port
150 Cabin air-conditioning intake (starboard wing only)
151 Wing root fairing
152 Wing front spar/fuselage attachment (tapered bolts/bushings)
153 Wing inboard rib mainwheel well recess
154 Wing front (No 1) spar
155 Undercarriage pivot
156 Hydraulic retraction cylinder
157 Auxiliary (undercarriage mounting) wing spar
158 Gun bay warm air flexible duct
159 Wing rear (No 2) spar
160 Landing flap inboard hinge
161 Auxiliary (No 3) wing spar inboard section (flap mounting)
162 NACA slotted landing flaps
163 Landing flap centre hinge
164 Landing flap hydraulic cylinder
165 Four 0·5 in Browning guns
166 Inter-spar gun bay inboard rib
167 Ammunition feed chutes
168 Individual ammunition troughs (350 rpg)
169 Underwing stores/weapons pylon
170 Landing flap outboard hinge
171 Flap door
172 Landing flap profile
173 Aileron fixed tab (starboard wing only)
174 Frise-type aileron structure
175 Aileron hinge/steel forging spar attachments
176 Auxiliary (No 3) wing spar outboard section (aileron mounting)
177 Multi-cellular wing construction
178 Wing outboard ribs
179 Wingtip structure
180 Starboard navigation light
181 Leading-edge rib sections
182 Bomb shackles
183 500 lb (227 kg) M-43 demolition bomb
184 Undercarriage leg fairing (overlapping upper section)
185 Mainwheel fairing (lower section)
186 Wheel fork
187 Starboard mainwheel
188 Brake lines
189 Landing gear air/oil shock strut
190 Gun barrel blast tubes
191 Staggered gun barrels
192 Rocket-launcher slide bar
193 Centre strap
194 Front mount (attached below front spar between inboard pair of guns)
195 Deflector arms
196 Triple-tube 4·5in rocket-launcher (Type M10)
197 Front retaining band
198 4·5in M8 rocket projectile

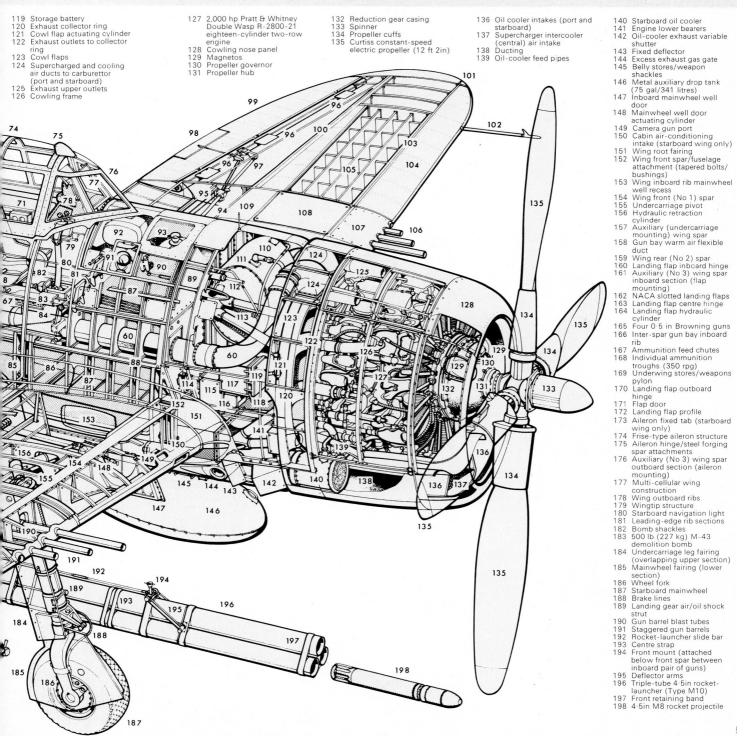

Vought V-166B F4U Corsair

F4U-1 to -7, F3A, FG, F2G and AU

Origin: Chance Vought Division of United Aircraft Corporation; also built by Brewster and Goodyear.

Type: Single-seat carrier-based fighter-bomber (sub-variants, see text).

Engine: (F4U-1) 2,000hp Pratt & Whitney R-2800-8(B) Double Wasp 18-cylinder two-row radial; (-1A) 2,250hp R-2800-8(W) with water injection; (-4) 2,450hp R-2800-18W with water-methanol; (-5) 2,850hp R-2800-32(E) with water-methanol; (F2G) 3,000hp P&W R-4360 Wasp Major 28-cylinder four-row radial.

Dimensions: Span 40ft 11¾in (12·48m), (British, 39ft 7in); length 33ft 8¼in (10·27m); (-1, -3) 33ft 4in; (-5N and -7) 34ft 6in; height 14ft 9¼in (4·49m); (-1, -2) 16ft 1in.

Weights: Empty (-1A) 8,873lb (4025kg); (-5, typical) 9,900lb (4490kg); maximum loaded (-1A) 14,000lb (6350kg); (-5) 15,079lb (6840kg); (AU-1) 19,398lb.

Performance: Maximum speed (-1A) 395mph (635km/h); (-5) 462mph (744km/h); initial climb (-1A) 2,890ft (880m)/min; (-5) 4,800ft (1463m)/min; service ceiling (-1A) 37,000ft (11,280m); (-5) 44,000ft (13,400m); range on internal fuel, typically 1,000 miles (1609km).

Armament: See text.

Above: Three-view of the F4U-1 (other sub-types similar except for armament or clipped wings).

History: First flight (XF4U) 29 May 1940; (production -1) June 1942; combat delivery July 1942; final delivery (-7) December 1952.

Users: (Wartime) Mexico, New Zealand, UK (RN), USA (Navy, Marines).

Development: Designed by Rex Beisel and Igor Sikorsky, the inverted-gull-wing Corsair was one of the greatest combat aircraft in history. Planned to use the most powerful engine and biggest propeller ever fitted to a fighter, the prototype was the first US warplane to exceed 400mph and outperformed all other American aircraft. Originally fitted with two fuselage and two wing guns, it was replanned with six 0·5in Browning MG 53-2 in the folding outer wings, each with about 390 rounds. Action with land-based Marine squadrons began in the Solomons in February 1943; from then on the Corsair swiftly gained air supremacy over the previously untroubled Japanese. The -1C had four 20mm cannon, and the -1D and most subsequent types carried a 160gal drop tank and two 1,000lb (907kg) bombs or eight rockets. Many hundreds of P versions carried cameras, and N variants had an APS-4 or -6 radar in a wing pod for night interceptions. Brewster made 735 F3A, and Goodyear 4,008 FG versions, but only ten of the fearsome F2G. Fabric-skinned wings became metal in the post-war -5, most of which had cannon, while the 110 AU-1 attack bombers carried a 4,000lb load in Korea at speeds seldom exceeding 240mph! In December 1952 the last of 12,571 Corsairs came off the line after a longer production run (in terms of time) than any US fighter prior to the Phantom.

Above: Rejected by the US Navy for carrier operations, the F4U-1 was flown aboard USS Essex in December 1944, by Marine Corps fighter squadron VMF-124.

Left: An F4U-1D, with twin tank/bomb pylons and rails for eight rockets, serving with a squadron aboard USS Essex in 1945.

Below: An F4U-1A, with hook removed, operating with 18 Sqn, RNZAF, over the Solomon Islands and Guadalcanal in early 1945.

Below: The Fleet Air Arm clipped 8in off each wingtip of shipboard Corsair IIs to facilitate folded stowage in the low-headroom hangers of RN carriers. They were first to operate Corsairs at sea.

Vultee 72 A-31 Vengeance

A-31 and -35, Vengeance I-IV

Origin: Consolidated Vultee Aircraft Corporation, Nashville Division; also built by Northrop Aircraft, Hawthorne.
Type: Two-seat dive bomber.
Engine: One Wright R-2600 Cyclone 14-cylinder two-row radial; (A-31, Vengeance I, II, III) 1,600hp R-2600-19; (A-35, IV) 1,700hp R-2600-13.
Dimensions: Span 48ft (14·63m); length 39ft 9in (12·12m); height 14ft 6in (4·40m).
Weights: Empty (typical) 9,900lb (4490kg); maximum loaded (A-31) 14,300lb (6486kg); (A-35) 15,600lb; (A-35B) 17,100lb (7756kg).
Performance: Maximum speed (all) 273–279mph (440–450km/h); initial climb, typically 1,200ft (366m)/min; service ceiling (typical) 22,000ft (6700m); range (typical) 600 miles (966km).
Armament: (A-31, Vengeance I to III) four 0·303in Brownings in wings, and two manually aimed from rear cockpit; internal bomb load of up to 2,000lb (907kg); (A-35A, Vengeance IV) four 0·50in in wings, one manually aimed from rear, same bomb load; (A-35B) same but six 0·50 in in wings.
History: First flight, July 1941; service delivery (RAF) November 1942; termination of production, September 1944.
Users: Australia, Brazil, India, UK (RAF, RN), US (AAF, Navy).

Development: Designed by a team led by Richard Palmer to a British specification passed to Vultee in July 1940, the Vengeance eventually became combat-ready in a different world. No longer was the dive bomber the unstoppable agent of destruction; by 1943 it was recognised to have value only in conditions of local air superiority, and even then to need fighter cover. Eventually 1,528 of all types were built, of which 1,205 were passed to the

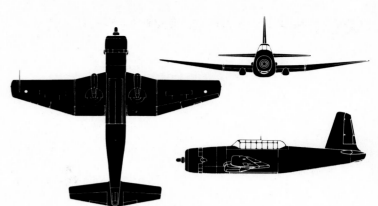

Above: Three-view, all sub-types being externally similar.

RAF (some purchased in 1940, others on Lend-Lease). Many served with the RAF, RAAF and Indian AF in Burma and South East Asia, where they at least saw considerable active duty. In 1940 it had been thought vast numbers would be needed, and a second production line was opened at Northrop, while the US Army adopted the type as the A-31. In 1942 the Americanised A-35 was in production at Convair's Nashville plant, but the US Army soon dropped even this version. Many RAF aircraft were modified as target tugs, and the last batch went to Brazil.

Right: Vultee built 831 aircraft designated A-35B with six wing guns and the R-2600-13 engine. None saw action with the US Army but 562 were allocated to the RAF and RAAF as the Vengeance IV. This one served on the Arakan (Burma) front with 7 Sqn, Indian AF.

Waco CG-4A Haig, Hadrian

CG-4A Haig; RAF name Hadrian

Origin: The Waco Aircraft Company; also built by 14 other companies.
Type: Assault glider.
Engine: None.
Dimensions: Span 83ft 8in (25·5m); length 48ft 3¾in (14·7m); height 12ft 7½in (3·84m).
Weights: Empty 3,790lb (1721kg); normal loaded 7,500lb (3405kg); overload 9,000lb (4086kg).
Performance: Normal towing speed 125mph (200km/h); typical speed off tow 65mph (105km/h); minimum speed 38mph (61km/h).
Armament: None.
History: First flight, early 1941; (production CG-4A) April 1941; final delivery, December 1944.
Users: Canada, UK (RAF), US (AAF).

Development: Though the vast US aircraft industry produced many types of military glider during World War II, the entire production effort was concentrated upon this one type, which was the only US glider to see combat service. In sharp contrast to Britain's larger, all-wood Horsa, the CG-4A fuselage was constructed of welded steel tube with fabric covering, the entire nose being arranged to hinge upwards for loading/unloading vehicles up to Jeep size, or light artillery. The side-by-side pilot stations hinged with the nose, the two control wheels being suspended from the roof. In the main fuselage were benches for up to 15 fully armed troops or cargo up to 3,710lb (5,210lb as overload). The wing loading was very low; there were no flaps, but spoilers above the wing to steepen the glide. No fewer than 15 companies collaborated to build the CG-4A, and in two years more than 12,393 were delivered. In 1943 an RAF Hadrian was towed in stages from Montreal to Britain in a flight time of 28 hours. A few weeks later hundreds were used in the invasion of Sicily. Several thousand were used in 1944 in Normandy and the Rhine crossing, while large numbers went to the Far East for the planned invasion of Japan.

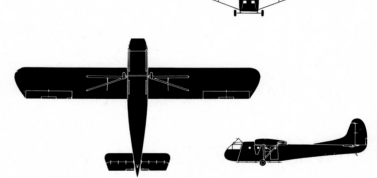

Above: Three-view of CG-4A.

Right: An armada en route for France on D-day, the tugs being C-47s. The photographer's tug is linked both by the tow-rope and a wrapped-around intercom link, seldom used on operational missions. One snag with the Waco, as with the British Horsa, was that collisions with even small obstructions, such as saplings, could stave in the flimsy nose and injure the pilots. In practice assigned landing areas often did contain both natural and enemy-made obstacles.